Called or Carried?

Developing Character in Leaders and Workers

Eric W. Davis

Soar Publishing LLC

**Called or Carried?
Developing Character in Leaders and Workers**

Copyright © 2013 Eric W. Davis

Unless otherwise indicated, all Scripture quotations are taken from the New King James Version, Copyright © 1982 by Thomas Nelson, Inc. Used by permission. All rights reserved.
All rights reserved. No part of this publication may be re-produced, stored in a retrieval system., or transmitted in any form or by any means-electronic, mechanical, digital, photocopy, recording, or any other-except for brief quotations in printed reviews, without the prior permission of the publisher.

Cover Design: Terry Croom
Editors: Sue Blackard
Sideana Pondexter
Published by Soar Publishing LLC
Columbia, S.C. 29229

　Library of Congress Catalog Number 2013957789
　ISBN 978-0-9888650-6-8

Printed in Canada
First Edition
0 9 8 7 6 5 4 3 2 1

Dedication

This book is dedicated to my Lord and Savior Jesus Christ. I don't intend this to be a cliché, it's simply the truth. He rescued me from Satan's oppression, my life of sins and, quite frankly, myself. Therefore, I owe Him my life. Second, I dedicate this book to my wife and soul mate Vanessa, whose love, grace and patience is a throwback to the character found in women of the 50's and 60's. She's a rare find in an age of sliding values and I'm grateful God put us together. My final dedication is to my three sons, Ezra, Elias and Emmanuel. They make me strive for more than manhood– because of them, I'm a father. I pray my example and sacrifices will help them to become even better men than their father. I love my wife and children more than they will ever know. That's the end of this dedication– God, my wife and my children.

Acknowledgements

I would like to first acknowledge the leaders who helped me come to maturity. The first is my own father, Pastor Eddie W. Davis, who taught me what it meant to become a man and more importantly, a man of God. He also licensed me to ministry and taught me the true character of a pastor. Eighteen years later, I'm still drawing from the lessons I learned from you, Pop! My late mother, Shirley A. Davis, was a leader in her own right. She was a community activist, social worker, politician, first lady and a best friend to the downtrodden. Her sacrifices for people everyone else would have thrown away taught me how to love and embrace the "lepers" of our society. Thanks Mom, I really needed that! I also want to acknowledge my sister Kim and brother Trent— much love to y'all. Thanks to my Aunt/Godmother Millie, who has been an inspiration to me since childhood— you always encourage me.

I have to acknowledge the pastors I've served under since I accepted Christ. First, Pastor Charles Jackson's ministry where I accepted Christ and experienced my first mega-church ministry. Thank God for Pastor Willie C. Barnes, through whose ministry in Eatonville, Florida I was later discipled in all forms of outreach ministry. Thanks to Pastor Ronald Critton, who served as Pastor Barnes' Joshua and my trainer, who taught me the real life lesson of "Follow the Leader." I'd like to acknowledge a friend and mentor in Bishop Phillip Davis who has been there when I needed a voice of wisdom. A host of ministerial friends should also be mentioned. Thanks to Dr. Andrew Thomas, my longtime friend and prayer partner. Also, to my spiritual twin brother Pastor Andrew Jones— keep "looking unto Him." Pastor Marcus Shiver— bless you and stay focused. Pastor Andre Barnes—God bless you my brother. Pastor Andrew Scott— keep serving and singing unto Him, brother. Pastor Ellis White— keep "kickin' chickin!" Pastor Greg Formby—

thanks for all the feedback. Pastor Robert Keene– stay strong brother. Elder Donte Lazarus– thanks for all of your help. To Bishop Vincent Collins– thanks for allowing me to sample the book with your leaders. Bishop Alvin McNair– your help on the church project was major. Pastor Johnny White–thanks for the kingdom support as well.

    I have to acknowledge the best church family on the entire planet earth in the form of Word of God Church and Ministries! I refuse to start naming specific people and break someone's heart, so I'll keep it general for love's sake. From ministers to deacons to members to the staff, I love and respect you all! You all inspire me to be a better pastor and leader and I pray this book will bless you. Let's keep on establishing God's kingdom on earth! To the rest of the WOGCM family– keep on striving! Pastor Keith Green and Baltimore WOGCM– welcome to the family, we love you! To Pastor Tito Hill and WOGCM Español– stay faithful. To our WOGCM pastors and churches in Ghana, Sierre Leone and Mexico– we love you and I look forward to seeing you soon. To my publisher, Elaine Smith– we did it and I always knew you would publish my first book! Bless you all and thanks for your support.

Table of Contents

1. Who is the Leader? 1

2. Follow the Leader 9

3. Called, Not Carried 17

4. Joshua was Moses' Minister 23

5. Fleeing Leaders 37

6. A Man Such as I 51

7. What Are You Chasing, Gehazi? 59

8. Five Stones….Five Enemies 67

9. Who Killed Uriah? 75

10. Thank God for Nathan 81

11. The Spirit of Diotrephes is in the Church 89

12. Who Will Give You Your Own? 99

1

Who is the Leader?

One of the most effective attacks of the enemy against the body of Christ actually starts from within the body. Rarely does the enemy mount an external attack against any single church that will disrupt progress and throw the church into turmoil the way one internal leader gone astray can. My 21 years of ministry and church experience have consistently revealed churches and pastors held hostage by followers used by the enemy to stop progress – whether it is hardened deacons committed to resisting pastors, to disgruntled associate ministers feeling their platforms are too small, to lay leaders murmuring about the vision and direction of the church. Find a church anywhere in this nation, and you will more than likely find the vestiges or collateral damage of this form of the enemy's attack.

Unfortunately, many leaders find themselves in situations where they are forced to prove who they are to the very people following them. In Numbers 12:2, we find Miriam and Aaron jealously questioning Moses' place with God. After the mind-blowing miracles and confirmations performed by God through Moses, can you imagine Miriam and Aaron even broaching the question of who God called to lead? Think about it. God spoke to Moses out of a burning bush, a flaming mountain and a thick cloud in the tent of meetings. In addition, God parted the Red Sea through Moses' outstretched hands, not to mention sending him back to Egypt (of all places, where he had committed murder) to confront pharaoh! After witnessing and hearing about all of this, Miriam and Aaron are found boasting to one another about God "speaking" to them as well.

It never ceases to amaze me how people create opportunities to tell what they believe God said to them but completely overlook all that God has **done** through the leader. Apparently, for some people the need to be recognized can override the manifested presence of God. *If God is speaking and manifesting Himself through a leader, why would anyone else "need" to be heard? Would this be God's need or the individual's?* As a matter of fact, in Exodus 4:13 Moses initially insisted someone else speak for God. God angrily obliged him by allowing Aaron to speak to pharaoh with Moses' "mouth." God told Moses, "I know that he can speak well." However, "I shall be with **your** mouth" and "**you** shall speak to him and put words in his mouth." God also told him, "**You** shall be as God to him." It was evident God had no interest in speaking to anyone other than Moses!

It is not often that the invisible God feels the need to make His presence as pronounced as He did with Moses, but when He does, you can be sure that it is a special moment in time and, at the very least, a unique person He has chosen. A person like this is so unique, in fact, that God Himself rehearses Moses' uniqueness in comparison to other prophets and asks Miriam and Aaron "why weren't you afraid of him?" God was not speaking of fearing the man but rather the unique relationship God had with the man.

When I hear people refer to ministers as reverend I often wonder if they understand the significance of the title. The Bible does not specifically refer to the title "Reverend" in scriptures but rather a reverence for God. Reverence is a form of Godly fear or respect for the authority of Almighty God. To call a man reverend suggests you have recognized the operation of God in him and hold him in this type of honor or "fear." To insult or offend him would suggest insulting God who sent him. Many people who use the title have not a clue of what they are saying. In many churches, they will call a minister reverend while they are fighting or plotting against him. In addition, they will call any pseudo minister in a suit "reverend" regardless of how unclean his life may be. It is blatant hypocrisy and though it may be birthed out of ignorance, in the end, God will not be mocked.

True spiritual leaders are a rare and minute breed among the billions of God's people who have existed. Of the millions of people referenced in the Bible, the total amount of actual leaders mentioned by name may only be in the low hundreds. However, leaders through whom God actually performed pronounced miracles like Moses were in the tens. They are essentially the rarest of the rare. Scripture sums it up as "many are called but few are chosen!" Matt. 22:14

A reverence for God operating in the leader is not only expected but also required. What God was essentially saying to Miriam and Aaron was "Moses is not a common man, handle him with care!" As evidenced by God's actions against Miriam, offending the leader whom God has chosen is considered an offense against God who leads him. God compares Miriam's insubordination toward Moses to an offense against her natural father. Not that Moses was her father – clearly he was her younger brother – but the insult aimed at him was received as one launched at the heavenly Father. So much so, the response of God was to "spit in her face" with leprosy for seven days (Numbers 12:9-14). Consider the aggressive and public nature of God's response to Miriam and Aaron for what seemed to be a relatively light situation. Why did it anger God and what can we learn from it?

The first thing we can learn from Aaron and Miriam's attitude and conversation is that it was far from insignificant in the eyes of God. In fact, it was downright luciferian or devilish at its core. What they did was akin to the attitude that eventually led Satan to rebel against God for the throne of heaven. It is dissatisfaction that takes hold of a follower's heart against a leader's position. These individuals typically believe the realm of authority held by the leader should be shared or transferred to them. No matter what the leader does, they believe they can always do it better.

Called or Carried? Developing Character in Leaders and Workers

One of the ways to discern a luciferian spirit is to expose the motive behind the action rather than the action itself. A pure-hearted follower understands that no single leader can do everything alone. Gaps in a system do not necessarily call for a change of leadership personnel but possibly the insertion of more followers to provide help. When pure-hearted followers see a vulnerable leader, they should look for ways to stabilize, not further destabilize them. A prime example of this was Moses' challenges during Israel's battle against the Amalekites in Exodus chapter 17. When Moses raised his arms, Joshua and the army were winning the battle. When he became tired and lowered his arms, the battle began to turn in favor of the Amalekites. Ironically, two of his followers, Aaron and Hur, were in the critical position to observe this trend. Aaron was an interesting leader whose character seemed to shift when paired with greater influences. In Numbers 12, he appears to follow Miriam's rebellious influence. Likewise, in Exodus 32, he is clearly influenced by the people's sin by making a golden calf. However, when paired with Moses, and in this case Hur, he tended to move in the direction of God. <u>He epitomized a leader who needed to be led.</u> Because Aaron's heart appeared to be pure at this time, he and Hur did not view Moses' fatigue as an opportunity to unseat him and test their own authority. They did not say, "Sit over there and rest and I'll take it from here." Instead, they seized the opportunity to sit Moses down in a place of authority and stood on their own legs holding his arms up for victory sake! It cannot be about whose doing the job or getting credit but rather that God is getting it done for all of us. In considering Aaron and Hur's actions, they did not only rest Moses' arms, they rested the man.

How much will you do to receive God's anointing? Now, how much are you willing to do in service of the anointing that is on your leader? Your answer to both of those questions will tell a lot about your character. Some people will go to any length to have the anointing of God upon their own life. Yet, amazingly, the same

R.T. Kendall — The Anointing

person will not have half the respect, enthusiasm or commitment toward serving when the anointing is on the life of someone leading them.

Do you respect the words of your leader enough to follow them? Or, do you believe God has given you greater words to speak to the Body? Are the words spoken by your leader insufficient? If so, are they insufficient for you, the people, or God? Who is more anointed to speak to the Body? If you, why didn't God choose you to lead?

Immaturity and selfishness cause individuals to view anointing like outfits, which can be adorned to make themselves look more attractive. Many people dream about being anointed and appearing powerfully blessed to everyone else. Anyone who has walked under the weight and authority of an anointing realizes it is often unattractive and far from fun. In fact, it comes with a burden to destroy the yokes in the lives of the people who surround the anointing. The truest form of anointing has less to do with the individual it rests upon and more about the people the individual is called to serve. Notice I used the word "serve" for the one whom the anointing rests upon because God's anointing is given to serve the needs of God's people. The so-called "five-fold ministry" is given for what I call the sixth element, which are the saints. From apostle to teacher, every one of the five-fold offices exists to equip saints. Unfortunately, immature people often look at God's anointing on a person's life and only see personal platforms, excitement and attention. Mature people look at the same person and see weight, responsibility and many struggles. So much so, these individuals feel compelled to do something to help the person who clearly is helping them.

In the battle against the Amalekites, Aaron and Hur were not only helping Moses, they were helping to save the lives of everyone in their nation. Twin brothers, Esau and Jacob, were declared by God to be separate nations while they were contending in their mother's womb. Amalek was the grandson of Esau. The Edomites (descendants of Esau) from which came the Amalekites, were all born to fight against and destroy Israel. With all of them stemming from Isaac's bloodline, the one thing that separated Jacob's or Israel's seed from Esau's was that the anointing and favor of God was present with Israel. This anointing was distinctly upon Moses the day the Amalekites ambushed Israel while they were traveling to the Promised Land. If the anointing had not been upon Moses, they would have certainly wiped out all of Israel, killing men, women and children. It was just that serious.

The Bible reveals, "The thief does not come except to steal, kill and destroy". John 10:10 The word "except" reveals the only purpose the enemy has for showing up is to perform one or all three of these acts. When the devil is present something critical will be missing, dying or falling apart. These are his three main forms of attack. One of the primary weapons that God gives His people against the devil is anointing. However, the individuals to whom the anointing is given are under a divine mandate to use the anointing for the sake of others and not only themselves. It is not to be played with because we are in spiritual warfare and lives and souls are at stake. If you desire anointing to build your own platform and promote your personal agenda, your character and immaturity will disqualify you from receiving it. You may be too immature for group leadership and would serve as a prime subject for satanic manipulation. As harsh as this may seem, I reiterate the fact that we are engaged in spiritual warfare for human souls. We are not playing a game, we are advancing God's kingdom!

Who is the Leader?

If you perceive yourself to be anointed, who are the beneficiaries? Does your anointing serve you more or others? How much does self-denial factor into your lifestyle? Whose yokes have been broken because you are anointed? Why do you desire an anointing? Do you believe you are mature enough to carry an anointing for others? Who is your leader and would they agree with you? If they do not agree, what does it mean to you? What do you believe your leader's opinion means to God? What if God and your leader are in agreement and you are not? How do you make the distinction?

2

Follow the Leader

Jesus stood on the shore of the Sea of Galilee looking at men who had the potential to perform "greater works" than He would do Himself. By His response to them, we assume He watched them toiling with their fishing nets trying to be successful at their natural craft. Realizing spiritual potential they could not see in themselves, He offered them a powerful and interesting proposal which began with, "follow me, and I will make you fishers of men."

The first two words of this statement are more than a request – they are a pre-condition. To achieve any of the spiritual promises or gain understanding, anointing and blessings of Christ, this one condition had to be met. No one in Jesus' inner circle could be considered a servant, friend, disciple or an apostle, for that matter, without meeting the primary condition of following the leader. It is a foundational principle for the development of anyone in the kingdom. Christ said to His disciples in Matthew 16:24, "If anyone desires to come after me, let him deny himself, take up his cross and follow after me." Anyone wanting to be with Christ must first deal with his or her inward desires. In our humanity, we do not desire to deny ourselves but rather gratify ourselves. Second, the persecution of the cross is not something we want but we "endure" it in obedience to Christ.

Now the third aspect is where our problems really arise – following Christ. We do not have the advantage of Christ audibly speaking to us in person, so we must trust His Spirit to speak through other men. Ultimately, following Jesus means we will have to follow another man's leadership. The apostle Paul admonished the Corinthian church to "follow him as he followed Christ."

In Matthew 28, Jesus left the model of disciples "making" new disciples, which means there are no self-appointed disciples. Everyone who comes to Christ does so by following the leadership of someone else. We cannot escape it because Christ mandated it! This principle does not diminish as we ascend in leadership; it intensifies. You cannot make yourself into a leader – the spirit of God is still developing leaders through human leadership.

In Acts 1, the disciples gathered in the Upper Room to determine who would fill Judas' vacant seat as an apostle. The primary qualifying condition was the individual selected had to have been present when Jesus was teaching. In fact, Peter said, *"Of these men who accompanied (followed) us all the time that the Lord Jesus Christ went in and out among us,"* which indicates no one outside of this condition could even be considered. Apparently, other men in addition to the twelve disciples quietly followed Jesus without titles or recognition. This attitude put them in a unique group of people qualified to become an apostle to the church. No mention of special gifting, anointing or power was discussed in the selection process, only the willingness to follow the leader. Matthias was selected to fill the twelfth apostolic seat of Christ, and the only thing we know about him is he always followed when Jesus was teaching.

Many people who are unwilling to submit themselves to God-sent leaders demand the right to have titles and prominent roles without meeting this basic condition of the church. A person who is unwilling or unable to follow leadership is actually dangerous to the health of the Body of Christ. Individuals like this are desensitized to the feelings and needs of others who are in the position of following someone. An individual gains a unique educational process when he allows his personal direction, destination and timeline to be under the responsibility of someone he is following. In short, every leader should learn what it feels like to be a follower by following someone else's leadership. Leaders who have not followed others successfully have the propensity to be

The Second Chair - great book

selfish. It is virtually impossible to know or care what a follower is feeling unless you have been in the position of following someone else. Following a leader is not only an experience; it is an education! This process creates a unique vacuum in a person's life which cannot be felt or experienced outside of the leader/follower relationship. Someone could stand right beside you watching the relationship develop and yet not understand the intimacy or idiosyncrasies associated with such a complex relationship. Your own spouse may not understand it if they are not following as well. You have to be inside the relationship to understand all of the dynamics.

As a novice minister, I once asked my pastor a series of questions about things I felt were easy to resolve. His response was profoundly simple, and I have never forgotten it. He said, "The view changes from the second seat to the center seat!" In short, when you sit where I sit, you will be able to see what I see! I discovered truer words were never spoken to me when I had my turn in the center seat. Old folks used to say, "You'll understand it better by and by!" Let us say "by and by" has come and I certainly understand better. I cannot fully quantify how much the second seat experience helped prepare me to pastor a rapidly growing congregation. I am grateful I was given the opportunity and education to follow before I was allowed to lead.

Have you trusted someone enough to follow his or her leadership? Do you struggle with following? Why? What have you learned from following other leaders? Do you consider following to be an educational lesson or a chore? What don't you appreciate about following? Why? What have you learned to benefit other followers?

When lead racecars begin to set a pace on a track, a vacuum effect is created for all of the cars which directly follow them. The aerodynamics of this vacuum is called a "draft." The pace-setting car penetrates the atmosphere using its momentum to overcome all unforeseen resistant forces, like strong winds or dangerous flying objects. In other words, the pace car does all the hard work and in effect creates a space directly behind them which drafts or carries the closest car behind it. The cars following the leader get the maximum benefit of the lead car's hard work. The closer the second car is to the lead car, the less resistance is felt. This is why during races you typically see the trailing car almost bumper to bumper with the pacesetter. Though both cars are traveling at an incredible rate of speed and covering an enormous amount of ground, the second car isn't working nearly as hard as the pace setter. The car following the lead is conserving fuel and reducing engine wear, yet going everywhere the lead car is going. The primary disadvantage for the second car is not being in the lead, but is this really a disadvantage? The lead car has the responsibility of not only leading but also carrying. However, the second car gains the critical benefit of knowing what it means to be carried. Successful leader/follower relationships are identical to this in ministry.

How close are you to your leader? How does having to follow a leader make you feel? Would you consider yourself to be in their draft or are you forging your own path? Are you waiting to get out of the draft and make your own pass? Or, are you enjoying covering a lot of ground with less resistance because of your follower position? What have you learned by being in your leader's draft? How do you think your experience will affect those who will eventually follow you? As a follower, have you become more or less sensitive to other followers? Has following grown you as a person or made you bitter?

The weight of pulling others with you as you seek to gain new ground is always a leader's burden. Until you are prepared to carry others even when it is inconvenient, you are not ready to lead. A good spiritual leader understands his ability and responsibility to carry others in his draft. Their momentum can take some people to places their own abilities and strength might be unable to accomplish. Therefore, equally as important as getting to the finish line is the knowledge of who you are carrying with you. Even as Paul "finished his course," he carried younger leaders like Timothy, Titus and Silas with him.

I have seen leaders move at such light-speed paces it is virtually impossible for anyone to be close to them. No one is essentially getting the benefit of being their disciple because they pace themselves to leave everyone else behind. However, when they get to their personal finish line they find themselves alone. There is no Peter to receive a Jesus type blessing for understanding the divine revelation upon which the work of the church continues. No John, who is close enough at the end of Jesus' natural life to receive the transfer of responsibility – "woman behold your son and son behold your mother." No Joshua to hear instructions from a dying Moses on leading the people into the Promised Land, or Elisha to pick up a fallen mantle after Elijah has made his transition.

No one is ever close enough to receive the benefit of the draft. In cases like this, the leader's primary concern is typically their personal well-being or prize. My personal observation of this type of leader is they either chose not or were never allowed to follow anyone else successfully.

> *If you are a pastor or leader, who is in your draft? Who is close enough to receive a transfer from you? Who can you shift responsibility to in your absence? If no one, why not? Is it your fault or theirs? Did your problem begin when you became a leader or did it start when you were a follower? Have you ever been a follower? If not, why not? Was it your leaders' fault or yours? Do you believe God agrees with your answers?*

When you are allowed to serve under someone's covering, it should produce a respect for both carrying and being carried in your heart. Realizing someone else is sacrificing parts of their life to help make you a better person and leader should make you more, not less, respectful of leadership. Too many followers believe they are doing more to help the leader than being helped. Racing is considered a team sport even though one person is driving the car. From the pit crew to individual drivers in separate cars, they may all be one racing team. In some instances, the trailing car following the pace car may be a team member. In this case, the role of the trailing car is to cause the pace setter to improve their speed and as a result improve both of their speeds and rankings. When trailing leaders think like team members versus competitors, all victories are shared. It is impossible for any racer to continually go around a track without any assistance. The driver who does not have a team and pit crew supporting him will break down and inevitably lose the race. As church leaders, we are not going to overcome our common enemy divided. Christ Himself said, "A kingdom divided against itself cannot stand." The stronger the opposition is toward the Body of Christ, the stronger our concerted efforts must be. Leaders and followers must work together to achieve common goals because it is the only way to achieve long-term success.

In world-class track meets, I like to watch distance runners

Follow the Leader

from nations like Kenya. Unlike runners from other countries, their runners quite often qualify in groups of two's and three's. Though they will most certainly have a lead runner on the team, they still train and run as a group. Track is unique in that a team of individual performers competes both as a team and as opponents for prizes. With the exception of relays, where four individuals compete as a team for a single prize, all others are competing for individual prizes. However, points are not awarded to the individuals but rather the team. Individuals receive prizes for personal performances but points are accrued to raise the overall team standing. The better the individual performances are the stronger the team becomes. Therefore, in world-class competition you have a group of individuals who have competed against each other to earn the right to represent their nation as a collective team. Ordinarily, they train on the same national team but compete against each other and runners elsewhere in the world to be considered the best. However, the Kenyans are not ordinary. Their runners are typically the best their underdog nation has to offer against the entire world and they realize they need each other. Wherever possible, they train and compete as a team running for a nation's honor, even in individual competition.

This is more difficult in sprints, but is clearly demonstrated when they run in packs during distance events. You rarely see great Kenyan sprinters – they are known for running the distance. While watching distance events, you will notice two or three of them bunched together at the head of a race setting the pace. It sounds like the racecar scenario but there are distinct differences. First of all, the lead runner early in the race is typically not the fastest teammate but the second or third fastest on the team. Using the same drag concept as racecars, the lead runner sacrificially works the hardest to maintain the strongest pace without burning out. He is called the "rabbit" and essentially does this for three quarters of the race. However, the true leader will run in the rabbit's drag conserving his energy. His strongest sprint or "kick" then comes in the last leg of the race. Opposing teams will perceive the rabbit to be the strongest Kenyan runner when he in fact is sacrificing himself to prepare the way for the leader. At the right time, their leader emerges from the pack trying to obtain a gold medal for the honor of their nation. His teammates made the necessary sacrifices in the race to insure him a clear lane to victory over their opponents. If their training and teamwork proves successful, they may sweep first, second and third places for their nation's top honor. If not, the sacrificial runners are content to not receive individual honors if it means their team comes away with the gold medal. This is self-denial and sacrifice at its best.

We can learn a lot from the Kenyan strategy in the church. First of all, though we are individuals contending for the eternal crown we are still a team. Like the Kenyans, the Body of Christ is a remnant in this world and though we are not underdogs, we also need each other. The honor of our kingdom is at stake in everything we do. Hebrews 11 reveals the faith patriarchs who ran the race before us and, like the Kenyans, sacrificed themselves so the church would gain victory. They are the great cloud of witnesses who motivates the church to run unselfishly with diligence toward a kingdom end. Even in death, they are still depicted as players!

How much of your individual efforts are for a team purpose? How much is personal? Would you be willing to sacrifice your personal victories if it means the team gets the glory? Are you willing to sacrifice yourself at a pace which benefits your leader more than yourself? How does it feel when you sacrificially work hard and your leader gets the glory and you get no personal recognition? Does it secretly anger you or are you genuinely happy? Would you let your team lose to gain personal recognition? How does it make you feel when your team fails vs. failing personally? How do you feel when the team wins vs. winning personally? Of these questions, which affects you the most – team or personal losses and gains?

3

Called, Not Carried

In Numbers 12:2, Miriam and Aaron are two leaders closest to Moses who not only question his personal life and decisions but his place with God as well. To try to qualify themselves as being used by God, they resorted to questioning Moses' choice for a wife. In spite of God's silence about Moses' choice, they apparently felt close enough to both God and Moses to raise their objections to His personal selection. Keep in mind, God is routinely speaking to Moses about the matters of His people and does not seem to raise this as an issue even when He has Moses on the mountain for forty days and yet, it is a major issue for the two leaders closest to Moses.

I have seen this pattern with followers desiring a lead role. They begin searching for some human or moral failure to disqualify or reduce a leader and subsequently promote themselves to a higher place.

If Miriam and Aaron believed they were qualified to be in Moses' place, why was his personal business even a discussion? Was it necessary to point out his perceived flaws for them to become qualified to fill his position? Here is a character question for all developing leaders. Does your spiritual promotion to leadership require someone else to be morally reduced from leadership?

If so, this makes you a leader by default not by promotion. If the person ahead of you has to decline for you to be raised up, you might not be as qualified as you think. If your pastor's gift has to be diminished or deteriorated for you to be recognized, you might not be as gifted as you perceive. True anointing does not have to campaign or lobby; it just reveals itself. Scripture reveals your gift will make room for you yet many people exhaust themselves trying to make room for their gift. Joshua, who was God's choice to lead the nation after Moses, never had to do anything but serve Moses. His personality and leadership was different from Moses' but he did not have to point out the differences to be recognized.

The people who have to point out these types of differences are typically campaigning for a spiritual spot. I have seen too many presidential election cycles where neither candidate has demonstrated great evidence why they should occupy the office. Instead, they fly around the country explaining why their opponent should not be elected. Consider this – we have so deteriorated as a nation, qualifiers for the highest elected office need only prove their opponent is worse. In effect, they are saying elect me by default. What is even sadder, our nation has become so void of character we embrace this madness! I would not hire a tutor for my six year old because they informed me another candidate was a criminal. If you have to disqualify someone to become qualified, are you the person for the job? Your individual character would still have to be qualified. This might work in a democratic political system but it will never be successful in God's theocratic system. Only God can qualify or disqualify His spiritual leaders.

If you as a follower believe you are being called to leadership, let me suggest a few character questions to ask of yourself, not your leader. "What can I learn from the one God has chosen to help me grow? What gift has God given to them that I clearly lack?

My experience has taught me that effective leaders usually have unique attributes, which may be difficult to duplicate, but can certainly be gleaned.

Another profound question to ask is what perspective has God given them that I am unable to see? It is frustrating to watch and listen to followers trying to authoritatively assess spiritual challenges and directions with limited information from both God and the situations at hand. Neither Miriam nor Aaron had been on the mountain with God to be briefed by Him, yet both of them felt qualified to speak for God concerning Israel's direction. There is no way you can fully assess what God is doing with His congregation from the bottom of the mountain. Your perspective is far too low. Until you are ready to make the difficult climb up the spiritual mountain to a place where God has chosen to reveal His will, you might want to assume you do not have a clear view to speak on some matters. **Notice, Moses was not carried to the top of the mountain by God, he was called up!** In other words, he had to physically grab hold of parts of mountainous rocks and properly place his feet to ascend to the place where God was satisfied to speak to him. He had no authority to determine how high he had to climb – that place had already been predetermined by God Himself. I imagine Moses with dirt between his nails trying to maintain his grip in awkward places. In my mind, I can see his feet digging into clefts of rock as he climbed higher for a revelation from God. If we had a clear view of Moses trying to climb the mountain of God, we might have gotten glimpses of him slipping or trying to maintain his grip. He was a man going through difficulties that are hard to imagine for the purpose of getting a clearer understanding of God's will for His people.

Being chosen does not make spiritual tasks easier; it is in fact harder in some cases. However, one of the things that keeps a leader through difficulties is the knowledge of being chosen by God. The thought "He chose me for this," may sometimes be the one thing to keep a leader climbing. Most people do not have a clue of the rigors involved in ascending to a personal and spiritual place where it pleases God to speak to you concerning His will for the church. Until God repeatedly calls you to climb out of your bed at three or four a.m. in daily intervals to talk about His business and decisions concerning the church, you might want to assume you do not have the best view.

Too many followers arrogantly make lofty assessments about critical spiritual moves with very limited perspectives of given situations. I did not say limited knowledge or information but rather perspective. We can have all the natural information and facts and still not have God's divine perspective. God will give His chosen servants divine perspectives which will alter negative conclusions derived from natural information. In 2 Kings, for example, Elisha and (we presume) his servant Gehazi awakened to find their camp was surrounded by the Syrian army. When Gehazi looked at the army through his perspective, he naturally found himself gripped by fear of eminent defeat and death. After all, how could two men, even God's servants, withstand an entire army? The information and facts collected in the natural realm were overwhelming and daunting. However, the prophet Elisha had an additional perspective. His view caused him to look beyond the natural army into a spiritual place. Surrounding the natural army on the hillside was an army of God's angels in fiery chariots. Two realities were coexisting for the moment, but only one could be seen by the naked eye. At any time the spiritual reality could have overtaken the natural reality. The angels could have defeated the Syrians while Elisha and Gehazi slept, only to awaken and find dead bodies or none at all. They could have been wiped out and the two servants not have known the battle even took place. Instead, God allowed them to wait until both Elisha and Gehazi were awake and walked outside to assess the situation. Immediately, Elisha's spiritual perspective gave him full assurance over the natural odds against them. Interestingly, Elisha's prayer was not for the angels to hurry and do what they were sent to do. Apparently, he was confident that God, who sent them, certainly knew when to release them.

Jesus told the disciples before His ascension, "it's not for you to know the times and seasons that God has set in His own authority." In other words, learn to leave God's matters in His own hands. It was God's job to fight the battle with the Syrians. Instead, Elisha used the opportunity to do his job which was to help grow and develop Gehazi. Elisha asked the Lord to "open his eyes" to the same spiritual perspective he had. Not his natural eyes, they were working fine. Actually, Gehazi saw the Syrian army surrounding them before Elisha did. Unfortunately, his spiritual eyes were completely closed. Good leaders have the ability to increase spiritual insight and understanding even in the midst of a crisis. However, it requires followers to respect their leader's perspective in lieu of natural facts. If Gehazi was unwilling to accept the fact that Elisha could see beyond him, he would have missed an incredible personal opportunity to grow spiritually. Elisha did not get this view on his own; he gained it by following the prophet Elijah. After Elisha's call, we read very little about him until Elijah's transition. Yet, he was following and being trained by Elijah. Unfortunately, many followers like Miriam and Aaron are more consumed with the opportunity to lead rather than their growth and development through following their leader.

Years ago, my community ministry work qualified me to be a candidate for an award offered by a national magazine. I flew to Tennessee, sat before a panel, and was grilled with questions about my work. It was smooth sailing until I was asked one critical question about myself. As I paused in the middle of the interview to think about the answer, my silence unfortunately became my answer. Inevitably, it cost me the award but taught me a valuable lesson. They simply asked me the same thing I will ask you. *Are you coachable or would you prefer God to develop you without human intervention? Who have you allowed to coach you through a crisis?* Many people in ministry want to become star players in the field of ministry without any legitimate coaching.

Do you value having a leader's perspective to guide you or do you feel your own perspective is enough? When given your leader's spiritual perspective, where do you place it with your own, above or beneath? Do you think questioning your leader's qualifications improves your standing with God? If your perspective is broader than your leader why would God allow you to follow them? What, if anything, are you supposed to glean from them? What has following them opened your eyes to spiritually which you didn't see before? If nothing, does the fault lie with you or them?

4

Joshua was Moses' Minister

We are introduced to one of the greatest leaders and generals in the scriptures receiving instruction from another one of the greatest leaders in the Bible. The word reads in Exodus 17:9 "Then Amelek came and fought with Israel at Rephidim. So Moses said to Joshua, 'choose for us men, and go out and fight Amelek'." The remainder of the scripture says, "so Joshua did as Moses told him, and fought with Amelek". From this point forward, his destiny was intertwined with Moses'. So much so, his ability to overcome or be defeated by the Amalekites is directly correlated to Moses' hands being raised or lowered on the mountain above the battle. How could one man's destiny be so closely related to another man's strength or weakness?

After Joshua defeats Amelek, God instructs Moses to do two specific things. First, record the victory in a book and second, recite it in the ears of Joshua that He (God) would utterly blot the memory of Amelek from under heaven. Apparently, Joshua received a divine promotion from God because of his obedience to God's servant Moses on that day. The next time we hear his name mentioned in the 24th chapter of Exodus he has been given the title of Moses' minister. As previously stated, this was clearly a divine promotion. He became the ministerial servant to the man whom God chose to usher in the first covenant. Joshua's willingness to serve in the roles given to him by God's leader qualified him beyond all other men to become the heir to Moses' leadership mantle. As Moses was being summoned to the mountain to receive the tablets of law, Joshua was the only man alive privileged to accompany him to the mountain of God. He was not allowed to climb the mountain with Moses but he apparently was content to wait at the foot of the mountain for forty days until the man of God returned. While Aaron was back in the camp making concessions with the Israelites, Joshua was at the bottom of the mountain waiting and, I imagine, praying for Moses. There is no telling what sounds were coming out of the divine cloud consuming the top of Mount Horeb but one thing is clear – when Moses descended the mountain, his minister was there. His selflessness and availability to Moses is a tremendous example to any aspiring leader. Joshua is not depicted as a man having received a tremendous gift of ministry. Instead, he is depicted as a man being a tremendous gift of ministry to Moses and Israel.

Unlike Joshua, one of the most difficult lessons for many followers to embrace is God sending them to be a gift to their pastor and church. As a result, it is never about a person using their gift, the person is supposed to be a gift! Whatever gifts a person has received from God; they do not belong to them for arbitrary personal use. The gifts belong to the Body of Christ and are to be subject to divinely appointed leadership. Just as Joshua served Moses, ministers are to become their pastor's minister. It is not about what they want to do in the church but rather what the leader needs them to do in the church. They are to make their abilities available for their leader's use.

This type of authority is not uncommon in secular administrations, which, according to Romans 13, receive their authority from God. I served on an advisory board for our local sheriff's department and learned, to my surprise, that deputies are employed at the sheriff's discretion. In other words, the deputies exist to serve the sheriff's needs. As they render service to the community and even place their lives on the line, they are effectively carrying out his administrative objectives. Should they cease to serve his objectives, they can be released at any time.

As a pastor, I see ministers come into the church all the time with visions of what they believe God wants to do with their personal ministry. I quickly bring them to the understanding that they do not have a ministry in the church. Be advised, the church belongs to Jesus but as a steward He gives the pastor a ministry to lead the church into divine vision. A ministry is an administration of gifts, workers and systems brought together to bring God's will to fruition. By stewardship, my ministry is currently leading Christ's local church and when God is finished with me someone else's ministry will take over. The church will remain until Christ returns but ministries will change. Individuals are not bringing ministries to the church they are submitting their gifts to the leader's ministry.

A big mistake that many lay leaders make is assuming ownership of a particular part of the ministry because their gift is the primary one being utilized. For example, I have staff ministers over prison outreach, evangelism, member care, facility operations, multicultural church, missions, etc. and every one of those ministries belongs to me by stewardship. No matter how long they do it or how many people are following them, they are in place to faithfully use their gifts in the ministries that pertain to the pastor's administration. Although Joshua was gifted and chosen to lead the army into battle against the Amalekites, it was not his authority in which God focused, it was Moses'. God was looking at Moses' hands held up on the hill, not Joshua's arms swinging in the battle below. In other words, God does not hold lay leaders responsible for the ministry – that weight belongs to the pastor. If something is wrong, off course with the vision, or displeasing to God it is still the pastor's responsibility to bring it back into divine compliance. The pastor's instruction overrides any idea individuals may have about how things should be done. I refuse to argue with someone about implementing the vision God showed me and holds me responsible for simply because their gift is being utilized.

When a lay leader's gift repeatedly becomes a nuisance or hindrance to the ministry, it is time to trust God to send a new gift. It is not ego-tripping; it is simply bringing divine order into contemporary terms and view. (Everything being done in the church pertains to what God has shown a pastor to include)– women's ministries, worship and arts ministries, children's ministries, elderly ministries and any creative thing developed to serve God's people. Everyone is pitching in their gift to be utilized in a broad ministry, which pertains to the vision given to their pastor. The scripture said Joshua was Moses' minister available to serve him in all capacities to bring Israel into God's promise. Just like Moses and Joshua, there are ministries and ministers given to pastors for the purpose of bringing God's church into all of its promises. Unfortunately, many churches, pastors and lay leaders do not operate under these divine principles and wind up with division and strife.

If you are a minister or lay leader in a church, whose minister are you? Who have you been presented to as a gift? Or are you waiting to facilitate your own ministry? Joshua was one of the clearest examples of a faithful minister in scripture, and we see his reward. He was allowed to do something Moses himself was not allowed to do. He had the privilege of leading God's people into the Promised Land. What an honor for a follower turned leader. It appears Joshua's character and consistency in serving Moses and the nation afforded him the respect and type of honor given to Moses as well. Many people want the respect and rewards but refuse to submit themselves to the criteria necessary to bring them about.

Not only did Joshua honor Moses in life but he and his leaders honored him in defeat and death as well. It is possible for a succeeding generation to make its distinctions from a former one and hit its mark without discrediting old work. Clearly, Moses and his generation of elders failed to hit the divine mark God had set for them by missing the Promised Land. The group of leaders surrounding Moses were fearful murmurers, sometimes double minded and often ungrateful. Scripture says, "Bad company corrupts good character" and we see a clear example of this in Numbers 20:10. At the complaints of the people, Moses sought God to draw water from a rock. Frustrated by the company of elders and people surrounding him, Moses disobeys God's instructions by striking the rock as opposed to speaking to it. He had internalized the negativity of his own leaders whom he deemed as "rebels" even as he was striking the rock. Their rebellion against God transferred to him.

It can happen to the best of us! We can become so consumed with people as pastors and leaders we can totally miss God's objectives while trying to satisfy His hard-hearted servants. In my lifetime, I have watched a generation of good pastors slowly pulled into compromising God's word for rebellious congregants who would not even follow Jesus Himself in the flesh! It is a generation of hard-hearted Christians who value traditions of men over the Word of God. Even when confronted with the Word, they show no deference or respect for its authority to govern their lives. Ironically, 1 Corinthians 10 reveals to us the "Rock that followed" the Israelites and subsequently Moses struck, was a picture-type of Jesus. Like the leaders of Moses' day, even when Jesus is directly supplying church folks' needs, they will still be ungrateful. The task of a great leader is not to become like the followers but rather they become like the leader. As great as Moses was, he failed in this task. His heart of compassion for a rebellious group of God's people caused him to lose his sense of sound judgment toward God's will. In a moment of heightened frustration caused by the bad-spirited elders surrounding him, he struck the rock of Christ twice when he should have spoken to it. He committed the ultimate offense against God, which sealed his own fate and the fate of those rebellious leaders who boosted him to do it. God said to Moses, "Because you did not believe in me, to uphold me as holy in the eyes of the people of Israel, therefore you shall not bring the assembly into the land I have given them."

How many modern pastors offend Jesus by trying to satisfy people who refuse to serve God with their whole heart? I wonder how many visions have been delayed or lost because of Moses-like disobedience? How could something that was seemingly so little cause such a great leader to miss his blessing? It is simple – disobedience! It is Moses himself who declares in Deuteronomy 28 that God will bless for obedience and curse for disobedience. We too, as preachers and leaders, are held accountable to obey the same instruction from God, given through us, to everyone else. There are no compromises or special exceptions! We cannot put our lack of belief in God back on unbelieving congregations. When the people refuse to follow the will of God, a hard line has to be drawn in the sand! The inability to acknowledge those lines is where I believe many great men like Moses have lost their direction.

As a leader, are you willing to take a hard stand when God's word is clear or do you compromise for people? Do you allow the complaints of people to cause you to shift your position in God? If the congregation is in one place and God another, where will you be? Are you willing to risk your compensation for your principles in God? What value do you place on the Bible's instruction versus ongoing traditions in your church? What are you willing to do about traditions which do not align with God's word? Will you do exactly what God tells you, even if it disappoints people? Have you allowed the rebellion of your congregation to get in your spirit? Has congregational lack of movement and rebellion toward God caused you to display anger toward God? Is your ministry moving toward God's promise or is it stuck in a place? Since you began leading the people, have they become more like you or you like them?

Here is where Joshua's leadership and Moses' are distinctly different. Given a similar set of circumstances Joshua emphatically tells the congregation to "choose whom you will serve" but "me and my house, we will serve the Lord!" No compromise from him – his instructions from God were clear. It is interesting that Joshua served Moses faithfully without internalizing the negative attitude and rebellion of the older generation. He honored them without becoming like them. Many young ministers believe honoring a preceding generation of leaders is doing exactly what they did. We have to be able to balance honor toward our leader's achievements with honesty toward their failures without losing the distinctions of our own assignments. Moses successfully led Israel out of Egypt and slavery, but he failed to lead them into the Promised Land. This is not an opinion it is a fact! This fact does not dishonor Moses; it only highlights the reality of Joshua's calling. It was Joshua's assignment to lead Israel into the Promised Land, which meant he could not do it exactly like Moses because Moses failed to do it.

There has to be sound-mindedness in succeeding generations about the successes and failures of predecessors. Doing the same things, which led to failure, is foolish! The fear of dishonoring the successes of previous leadership has crippled many contemporary churches and pastors. The inability to admit shortfalls while acknowledging areas of strength is often difficult. Many new pastors are afraid to make necessary changes because congregations feel it is offensive to a previous leader's legacy. It is absurd to think nothing will change with the inception of new leadership. No one leader will get it all done nor will he get it all right! Jesus was the only leader to get it all right, but even He did not get it all done. Christ laid the foundation but He plainly told the disciples they would "do greater works" after He ascended to the Father. Clearly, Joshua understood this and made the necessary changes to cause his leadership to be successful. However, he did not destroy Moses' legacy in the process, he simply established his own. Moses' legacy involved God speaking to him and he spoke directly to the people. Somehow, his generation of elders seemed to wind up distanced from him and often stood in error with the congregation. How often have we seen this in the contemporary churches? The pastor is in one place while the other leaders are in another position waiting on him to convince them rather than lead them. Joshua, on the other hand, spoke to God then according to Joshua 1:10 "commanded" the leaders to repeat his instructions to the people. This sounds like a different style of leadership than Moses' to me!

I sometimes watch young Joshua-generation pastors make one of two mistakes. Either they make Moses-style elders of a fresh new generation of leaders or they make new rebellious leaders who work to discard anything that has a semblance of being old. It is frustrating to watch a generation of fresh young leaders trying to use the same old style and voice of previous leadership.

Every person is given a gift and a unique voice to be used for God's glory. Even if individual gifts are similar, voices are certainly different. By voice, I do not mean tenor, tone and sound but rather one's sphere of influence. Some voices are raised by God to call, reach and lead people that another voice would never reach. As hard as many contemporary pastors may try to imitate it, Martin Luther King Jr.'s voice has been silenced. Another voice of influence will certainly be raised, but it will not be his. Mimicking King's voice will not produce the same sphere of influence because the times and people are different. At some point God's revelation that "Moses my servant is dead" had to be accepted by the Israelites and subsequently they had to move on from that place. There has to be an appreciation for the unique influence of one voice while holding out the expectation for God to raise another.

At Pentecost, 120 people were all gifted in the Upper Room but each of them had a distinct voice to reach different people below in the streets. There was no place for mimicking – it was vital that each voice was raised to draw the 3,000 people God purposed to reach. Many fresh new souls are missed when young Joshua leaders choose to silence their own voices of influence to sound like Moses. Not only will it not compel people, it is a turn off! People with real issues desiring changes in their lives do not want to listen to an echo or parrot of someone else's voice. It simply will not fill their need. They would rather continue their search for a real voice or wait until the voice finds them. Mimicking leaders typically cannot do fresh works with new people because their voices do not lead in new directions. At best, they become good maintenance men or custodians of a former pastor's vision. Frustrations within the congregation will typically arise because though there is a form of new leadership, younger generations feel like they are essentially wandering with Joshua as they did with Moses. In cases like this the leadership surrounding Joshua will typically consist of a mixture of older and younger men who reflect the same attitudes and spirit of a former generation. They usually cannot move forward because the voice, which influences them, is more reflective than progressive. As a result, they mark time while reflecting on what has been rather than what will be.

Year after year, congregations like these celebrate their deliverance from Egypt under Moses with no real hope of obtaining a Promised Land following Joshua. The ministerial highlight of the year is usually an anniversary service honoring their former glory days. Long services are held reflecting on the mighty works performed by Moses to deliver the people from slavery. Then, when the service is over, the saga of wandering in a present wilderness continues! The only forward momentum to be found is quickly joining the planning committee to make the next anniversary another "smashing" success. What a tragic waste of divine purpose, potential, gifts and might I add, voice! Paul describes those consumed with the former glory of the old covenant in 2 Corinthians

3 as a "veil which comes over people's hearts whenever Moses is read." He said, "The people's minds became dull" because they essentially could only see God's glory through the faded former glory of someone else!

As a leader, are you progressive or reflective? Whose voice of influence do you speak with, yours or someone else's? How do you balance respect for those who have led before you versus that which you are led to do? What do you honor the most – your assignment or their legacy? Are you honest about their successes? How about their failures? How do you respond as a leader to the area where they failed? Who are you afraid of? Why? What can they do to you? Are the consequences more important than God's call on your life? If you are an aspiring leader, which type of leader do you think you would become? Why?

In contrast, we have developed a fresh new "throw everything away" generation. This type of leadership believes anything which remotely reflects being "old" is inherently useless. Modern Joshua, in this case, wants to throw away anything Moses used, did or even left behind, including the people! It comes off as extremely rebellious and disrespectful because the central focus is Moses' failures as opposed to his successes. It is the polar opposite of the previous scenario where Moses could do no wrong. In this case, nothing he did was right. The fact that God used him to deliver slaves from Egypt, and the people's deliverance was a result of his sacrifices and leadership, becomes irrelevant. The central focus becomes getting away from the place we are in, no matter what we leave behind! Nothing is deemed to have enough value to carry with us. It is an immature, selfish form of leadership, which will eventually be confronted by its own mistakes. One can only reap what we have sown and become partakers of that which we have produced. If we produce rebellion and disrespect in people, it has to return to us!

One of the primary mistakes of this type of modern Joshua leadership is discarding the long developed values of Moses' generation. Unlike those who cling to the practices of a former generation, this group too easily discards old, seasoned values for new fluff. Never destroy foundations, build on them. This trend has unfortunately become apparent in our preaching, worship services, music and certainly our lifestyles. How could "new" church come out of and stand on the shoulders of the old and not respect any of the foundational values that raised us? After all the scripture does say, "Honor your father and mother that it may be well with you." To discard without respect is not honor— it is dishonor. For example, we have discarded with extreme prejudice and disrespect valuable parts of worship like hymns. Many of our contemporary singers and musicians neither know how to sing or play them. Yet, they find ways to introduce and blend any "new" popular secular song into worship. I am not suggesting we sing them every week, but how can timeless spirituals and hymns written and sung by Christians no longer be appropriate in contemporary worship? Yet, ungodly secular music intended for clubs and parties are preferred and frequently sampled! Some Christian artist will introduce entire secular songs lyric for lyric and note for note with no changes.

Can that which led us into sin lead us into the presence of God simply because it changed venues? How can we love God, hate His music and love the world's music at the same time? Did not John teach, "He who loves the world does not have the love of the Father?"

> *Why is the Bible becoming less relevant in preaching than contemporary principles and ideals? As this generation continues to drain the church of the core values that saved us from spiritual slavery, how long will it take to throw baby leaders out with the old bath water? Will modern Joshua be able to resist his own generation's rebellion when they decide to throw him away as they did Moses?*

One of the primary tricks of following secularism is its trendy nature, which holds no allegiance to anything that does not satisfy its lustful desires. It does not abide in God's love but rather a self-centered lust, which is not concerned about anyone else's preservation. If a leader and church lives by secularism, they will die by it. Paul told the Galatian church, "If you bite and devour one another" you will "consume one another." I am afraid we are quickly developing a contemporary church whose appetite for the wrong things will eventually cause it to consume itself. *As new leadership continues to lead churches to discard old values and consume new carnality, what will the future church become?*

The wisdom of Joshua and his leaders enabled them to blend old values with new directions. They paid homage to the successful things, which Moses taught them about serving God; improving upon the failures which caused the generation to miss their promise. They did not have to destroy the previous generation, just move past the place of wandering. Somehow, Joshua was able to be Moses' general, minister and his successor without compromising any of his roles. He had to equally respect Moses in death as he did in life. It was not only Moses' legacy at stake but Joshua's legacy as well. He could not allow his legacy as a leader to destroy his legacy as a follower. Neither could he allow his legacy as a follower to hinder the call and direction of his leadership.

The distinction of Joshua's generation of leaders is that they *why Joshua did not have the grumbling Moses had to deal with*

Joshua Was Moses' Minister

declared they would be with him as they had been with Moses. This younger generation did not carry the spirit of their elders that had fought and resisted Moses – they received him as their leader. The difference is, they were not Moses' leaders, they were his followers. Moses and his generation of leaders were now dead and these were newly emerged leaders. They were equally prepared to follow Joshua as they had Moses. Therefore, they did not need to be led by negotiations, they wanted a leader! They told Joshua to be strong and courageous and whoever did not obey his commands would be put to death! After wandering forty years with their parents, they had a mind to enter into what God had promised, even if it meant killing their own! That is a strong but necessary commitment if you are to become one of God's leaders. The word commands us to set aside all relationships and even our own life for the cause of Christ. Unwillingness to do so is deemed as being "unfit" for real kingdom work. However, the prime objective is not to discard anyone but lead everyone into the promises of God. It does however require Joshua-like wisdom, which knew how to bring the old and new together.

How much value do you place on "old" standards? Are you of the mindset that anything old needs to be changed? Why? Do old standards and values cramp your style of leadership? What is your style of leadership? Do you believe your style is holy in God's sight? Is it possible to accomplish your objectives without destroying old standards? Where and how did you gain the wisdom to lead? Does any part of your leadership pay homage to someone who led you? How do you honor their leadership through your own? Given the opportunity to lead, are your new standards more or less righteous than the old are? How do you know? If you are wrong, what do you believe will be the impact? Are you prepared to accept it? Are you sure?

5

Fleeing Leaders

Most people who flee from responsibility in the midst of major crisis have had patterns of running from circumstances all their lives. Essentially, when anything of significance challenges them, it raises up a fleeing versus overcoming spirit. Evaluate their history and you will often find they ran from relationships, jobs, business ventures, educational pursuits, friendships, churches and primarily, strong church leadership. This type of person's resume' will typically have many incomplete experiences with interesting reasons why they "had" to leave situations unfinished. In addition to running from incomplete challenges, they quickly run to anything that appears to rescue them. Runners rarely take the time to evaluate the consequences their actions have on the ones they leave behind. They are only interested in saving their own skin. At a challenging time when a runner is needed to dig in and lead, be prepared for them to find or create a reason to leave. Jacob began his adult life as a runner. Being born with a deceptive nature, as his name means "supplanter", it did not help him to have a mother who fostered his deceit. When they deceived his dying father and twin brother out of the firstborn blessing, given the choices of confronting his actions or running, he chose to run. He began his adult life running from his own deceitful mistakes to a place where he expected to be rescued.

One of the worst things to happen to a runner is to believe that fleeing from a challenge is really the best option. Upon arrival at his relative Laban's house, he discovers the woman of his dreams and begins a seven-year chase to have Rachel as his wife. He gets a dose of his own medicine when Laban deceives him and instead gives him his older daughter Leah on the wedding night.

He desperately wants Rachel as his wife, and spends another seven years pursuing her while being married to a woman he does not want. Running between his desires and his reality, he births children with Leah, none of whom has his focus, while he is working to establish his vision with Rachel. It is often difficult for runners to stabilize or settle their personal lives when they have dreams of future prizes. They have the tendency to neglect core responsibilities while in pursuit of a dream because they believe the obtainment of the prize will fix everything.

Do you justify neglecting present responsibilities to reach future goals? Are you comfortable leaving things unfinished? Would you deceive people if you believe it is necessary to get what you want? What is your response when confronted with your own mistakes?

Truly stable leaders have to struggle to find and learn balance in their lives without leaving essential pieces too far behind. Bringing a wife and children along for the ride on a God assignment may require many unplanned stops along the way. If I drive thirteen hours to New York from South Carolina by myself I may only stop to get gas, eat or use the restroom two maybe three times. If I take my family with me, I have to prepare for quite a bit more stops as the need arises in them. If I were rushing, it would be frustrating to bring my family with me. Bringing them along would require me to travel at a different pace with a different mindset. Runners cannot handle the pressure of bringing people along with them who cannot handle their pace. They do not have the patience to make the necessary stops along the way, and drive the people with them too hard, long or fast.

So was the case with Jacob. After Jacob has eleven children with Leah, Rachel and a couple of hand maidens, he is ready to

Fleeing Leaders

run again. Laban convinces Jacob to stay, and the two devise a plan for Jacob to develop his own land and livestock. When Jacob's endeavors prove successful, it raises conflict with Laban and his sons, and once again, the primary option for Jacob is to flee. Realizing he was going to run regardless, God intervenes and directs him back toward his homeland. When the right opportunity arises, the scripture says, "**He fled with all he had**." There is a significant problem, however, with Jacob's flight at this stage of his life. At this point in his life, he is no longer young and he is not alone. He has now become the father of a large family, with various wives, baby mamas and many possessions he is responsible for leading. He has become the epitome of a fleeing leader. His fears, paranoia and unresolved character issues from his youth caused him to move at a pace far too fast and detrimental to those who were following him. To make matters worse, Rachel was pregnant at the time with Benjamin, their twelfth child.

How much does your childhood factor into your leadership? Do you believe you have any unresolved issues? How has your character changed in adulthood? What effect have immature decisions had on your family, ministry or anyone following you? Are you continuing old patterns or changing them? How do you know? Would your family and others who follow or serve with you agree? Would God agree?

I had a professor who held the philosophy that a class could only move as fast as its slowest student did. Therefore, he stopped to answer any menial question as long as everyone arrived at the final destination together. He did it because he valued the responsibility given to him to move a group of people from one place of understanding to a higher one. This might not be a commonly accepted practice but it is certainly a noble approach for anyone leading a group of people. At this point in Jacobs's life, his character was far from noble. The pace he chose was all about getting himself as far from his trouble as quickly as possible. He was still stuck in the mindset of saving his own skin. Because of his selfishness, he had no idea the effect this pace would have on the feeblest ones who followed him.

I sometimes watch and listen to fleeing pastors who have been called to be under shepherds of Christ flocks. If you pay attention, their less-than-noble areas of character often give them away in conversation. First of all, they often are far too preoccupied with God dealing with them personally rather than the people they are called to lead. You will hear things like, "God is calling **me** to more than this" or "calling **me** to another level." The language is usually not about growing the community through meeting people's needs or developing their faith. It is usually a tone of more coming to launch the individual higher and subsequently leave everyone else behind. They view themselves as rockets and the members as launching pads. Any opportunity to advance this type of leader personally will send them in flight. They will chase a personal opportunity to the end of the earth with no regard for who they are leaving or dragging along. If they cast a vision and get everyone motivated and vested, they will run if they hit a tough spot or discover a better personal opportunity. They may not leave physically; it may only be in focus.

How many people have been left holding the bag in incomplete visions because a fleeing leader was stuck and slid his way out of the situation? Have you ever experienced a leader leaving a vision incomplete? How did it affect you spiritually or emotionally?

Fleeing Leaders

If you are a leader, have you ever done this? How did it affect you as well? Have you ever put your desires before God and His people's needs? Why? If you had to abandon something, did you consider all sides before doing it? Why or why not?

Fleeing leaders will start moving in a direction, see something more appealing, then turn and run in a new direction, leaving everyone else in the dark and incomplete. In anxiety, they may also go after something so hard and fast, they will kill the members and leaders who are following them. By killing them, I mean they will give no consideration to the people's personal time, finances, relationships, jobs or spiritual development. The only thing that matters is pursuing whatever they want done in the shortest period. As a result, they may even kill the people they love the most and are closest to them. Jacob's pace eventually proved to be too much for Rachel in her pregnancy. Running alongside him in his desperate endeavors finally overwhelmed her and she died giving birth to Benjamin. Aside from noting where she was buried, there is no mention of any significant grieving for her on Jacob's behalf. A fleeing leader will drive you to death, take the thing produced through your life struggle, bury your efforts and keep running. A progressive leader has to continue moving, but has no issue with paying homage to the efforts of those who helped him arrive at a destination.

How do you pace yourself as a leader? Do you consider the weaker who follow you? Do you feel responsible for them? Do you believe they are strengthened or hurt by your leadership? Are you more concerned about them or yourself? If yourself, why should they follow you?

I have seen too many good people die in spirit following leaders who are running behind pipe dreams. The members who follow them quite often become discouraged with their entire Christian journey and like Rachel wind up cursing innocent things. As Rachel was dying, she named the baby Benoni, which means "son of my sorrow". Jacob however, renamed the child Benjamin which means "son of my right hand". People dying spiritually lose their ability to see good in their own lives and others after following fleeing leaders down too many trails to nowhere. They have a tendency to curse newly developed visions and concepts with the negative language of their vantage point. Having seen so many incomplete places in their own lives, everything becomes a new adventure to nowhere.

I have received people like this into our ministry not realizing the depth of their pain and discovered it can frustrate a vision and visionary. You find yourself trying to bring a member along with your vision but they are determined not to follow. By this, I mean they have become so discouraged with uselessly following people they refuse to become enthusiastic about any more visions. In effect, they unconsciously hold the ones who are actually trying to help them, responsible for all those who left them. Church becomes more of a routine than an actual relational experience with God and His family. You cannot "get rid" of this type of person because pushing them away would be equivalent to leaving them. I have discovered they can come along for the ride but they are usually not good for leadership. One can only lead someone else where they are going, and until they are healed that is usually not forward.

People like this require a lot of time and attention because, ironically, their comfort zone is typically close to leadership. Inevitably, they will move close enough to your leadership team to become a distraction of inactivity. From afar they look the same as the fig tree that misled Jesus. Like Jesus and the tree, upon closer observation they make you feel like cursing them as well because of their lack of fruit or productivity. However, they are people, not trees, and deserve an opportunity like another fig tree mentioned in scripture, to be dug around and fertilized. To curse them, is to become like them in your perspective. They have to be moved into adopting your fresh vision and direction as opposed to your taking on their cynicism. It requires patience and truth to help a person like this heal. They have to be reminded your ministry did not do them harm and cannot be held responsible for other's actions. In short, they will have to grow past it. Until they do, they should not be given the authority to speak over living things because they may speak out of their personal sorrow as Rachel did.

Have you ever been inactive in a new place because of old hurts? What was your rationale for doing this? Have you ever lost the desire to receive a new vision? Why? Who or what discouraged you into this place? Have you ever felt like something died in you spiritually? How did you come out of this place? Are you still in this place? Can you trust anyone else to help you? What are your fears? Would you consider yourself optimistic or cynical? Would your leader and others around you agree? How fruitful are you now? Why?

Fleeing leaders like Jacob typically cannot see themselves until they are made to see themselves. A combination of God, failed endeavors, and mounds of good people lost are usually in the equation required to wake them up. In the end, a fight between God and the runner is required. In Jacob's case, the dread of going back home to face the deceit committed against his brother, Esau, was more than the fleeing leader could handle. In varying degrees, he exposed everyone else trying to preserve himself. Before he personally confronted his own mistakes, he openly sacrificed the women and children in his life by putting them in danger. At the end of it all, he was in the most secure position of everyone.

Many contemporary leaders are guilty of the same kind of cowardly actions. They care so little about the people around them, they will put them in more vulnerable positions than themselves. They cast grand visions and place higher financial burdens on the people than on themselves. Like Jesus said of the Pharisees in Matthew 23, "They bind the people with heavy burdens but they themselves won't lift a finger." True men of God are the first to take on the challenges of divine sacrifice for God's will to be done. Jacob's deceitful and callous attitude required a showdown with God. The runner had run out of places to go. There he was, across the brook, presumably alone and separated from enemies and loved ones. Then the angel of the Lord showed up when he had nowhere and no one else to whom he could run. He was all alone! This divine showdown is not only about him contending with God's will for his life but his own pitiful character as well. In the conflict, the angel raises the question of what he calls himself. "What is your name?" he asks him. By answering the angel as "Jacob," it means he still thinks of himself as a deceiver. Here is the real problem!

What is your personal perspective of yourself versus God's vantage point? In other words, does God agree with your view of self? Truth be told, our internal fight will not end until our external view of self is changed. Too many leaders are fighting hard to make themselves successful primarily because they have a distorted view of themselves. Only when we release our egos and poor character habits do we discover the struggle has never been about becoming successful but rather being holy. When holiness is pursued and obtained, success will be present because holiness is the divine attribute of God. Therefore, the success achieved is beyond anything we could think to ask or imagine because it is totally divine. We arrive at a place of success with God Himself because we accept what He wants for our lives over our own ideas. Everything else is redefined by what He declares us to be. It is a divine manifestation of His word spoken over our lives. He says, "No longer shall you be called Jacob your name is Israel." We see a man wrestling with God, but the Father saw the character of a nation coming into existence. It appeared the character of a man had to be broken, but we now understand the spirit of a nation had to be formed. Now comes one of the most important pieces to the puzzle – no more fleeing in his life.

It is amazing how God will position us where we cannot go back to old natures and habits even if we try. In the redevelopment of our character, He will also deform old attributes, which formally led us out of His will. For example, thieves find it impossible to steal and it is no longer easy for liars to tell lies when God puts His hands on us. God does not always deform us but He will allow it. He allowed Paul to be saddled with an affliction to keep him from becoming conceited. Something about the touch of God deforms areas that formerly displeased Him while bringing to life things that laid dormant. When He finishes, even fleeing leaders are unable to run anymore. When the angel touched Jacob's hip socket something shook loose and changed his natural walk therefore impairing his ability to run. As sure as his natural walk changed, so did his character walk. Israel, the man, would now face everything Jacob had done and fled from. A different man re-emerged from the solitary place on the other side of the brook. It was impossible for this new man named Israel to flee from facing the long path of Jacob's deceit, even if he tried. The time had finally come to face Esau for the deception Jacob had done in the past. As the sun rose over Penial, a new man named Israel limped in his brother's direction. Whatever lied ahead of him, running away was no longer an option. He had to face his past like a man who had spent time with God and himself.

What is your personal view of self? What experiences have shaped this view? Have you wrestled with your old versus a new nature? Who has emerged from this experience? Have you had a Jacob to Israel moment? Are there any old natures God has deformed in you? If you have not wrestled with God and self, why not? Do you believe you do not need to change? Does God agree with you?

Like Jacob, en route to becoming the person and leader God calls us to be, we wrestle with a lot of character development moments. When the fleeing spirit is broken in us, we have no choice but to confront ourselves through the eyes of God and others. However, it takes maturity to walk out the corrective process of our own spiritual and character flaws. Believe me, we all have them. At some point, running from our mistakes and blaming others is no longer an option because too much of our past has caught up with us. Our actions begin to scream louder than our words. We become known by what we have done regardless of preaching, teaching, ministry size or other gifts.

Unfortunately, we can become Satan's best character witness against the Kingdom if we are not careful. The truth is, many leaders are afraid to go back and confront the people we have betrayed or let down in the past. It is not an easy thing to do but if you want to prosper in God, it is necessary. It demonstrates a sign of genuine maturity and growth in God. I have seen too many ministers and their wives wreak havoc in a church on their way to starting their own ministries. After leaving destructive paths like Jacob, they take off running when the time seems right for them. Somehow, these types of individuals believe starting a church erases all the hurt and dirt they committed in places they left.

My pastor once told me a pastor will receive the same type of member he was to someone else. It sounded like the Bible to me.

Fleeing Leaders

"Whatever a man sows, that he will also reap." Gal. 6:7 Truer words were never spoken to me. I have been blessed with a great group of people serving **with** me, and I believe it is due in large part to the service I rendered to other churches. I had no hidden agendas or deceit, I served and helped in whatever capacity I was allowed. I can return to those churches without a trail of lies, bad blood and character cover-ups. As a result, I can honestly say, for the most part, I have seen and pastored people like myself for the past thirteen years.

Deceivers, liars and divisive people are destined to try to lead people like themselves as well. Notice I said, "try" because they will be no more successful at pastoring "themselves" than others were. Our church has grown from tens to thousands over the past decade and I have watched my share of Jacobs come through and do their stuff and flee. Inevitably, they try to replicate the ministry they refused to submit to and wind up failing miserably. It never does materialize into what they expected because they lack the key character and righteous components to build a successful ministry. The character is not only lacking in themselves but will not typically be found in the type of membership they draw to their churches. Snakes brood with snakes while lions form a pride with other lions. The reluctance to go back to former leaders and admit their immaturity and sin after becoming unsuccessful as leaders essentially seals their fate. God allows the very church they conspired and manipulated to have to become a burden and a curse to them.

Churches like these will never find sustained peace until the corruption in the leadership is resolved. It cannot truly be resolved without involving the offended parties of their past. Scripture says, "If you have an ought with your brother, go to him." Matt. 5:23 (KJV) You do not have a character-changing encounter with God without Him leading you back to the Esaus you have offended in your life. Fulfilling this scripture requires a heart reformed by God as well as flesh deformed by Him. Pride and egotism have to be destroyed and discarded in Kingdom trash cans. Clearly, this is not a job for Jacob – it is the prime responsibility of Israel. Only a man who has received a new outlook from God will place the value of going back down his former paths of destruction. Men who lack character will devalue the need to do it, citing God knows what is in their heart. I agree that He does, and it is exactly why He sends us to our offended brothers. Only the man who obeys God will discover He has already prepared the hearts of offended people to receive Him.

We have to be poured out or emptied of our issues if we are to be effective in our calling. It is interesting to note that Jacob had to cross the Ford of Jabok which means to "pour forth." Part of being effective as Israel was being emptied of Jacob. The selfishness and deceitful character which carelessly wrecked other's lives and harbored no concern for their outcomes had to be poured out completely. Israel would become responsible for shaping the nation, which God would use, and they did not need the leaven of Jacob exploding in their character. As leaders, we not only pour God's word into others but also our attributes as well. People look for individuals to follow and imitate as Paul instructed the Corinthian church to be imitators of him. If leaders do not effectively empty themselves of their baggage, the people they draw to their ministries who are not like them will eventually become like them. Jesus said the Pharisees would "travel land and sea to find one proselyte and would make them twice as much a son of hell" as they were. People who have produced hell in other's ministries will continue to produce hell in members of their own church. According to Philippians 2, Jesus emptied Himself and made Himself of no reputation but took on the form of a bond servant.

Amazingly, Christ produced servanthood in His disciples because of the pure servant's heart in Himself. Here is God's Son, who had every right to be served, giving up His royal privileges that He might serve others. Moreover, He "took on" the form of a bondservant which means the Son of Man did not come to be served but rather to serve others. It reveals that Christ was not only intentional about completing His assignment but in how He completed it as well. It is also important to recognize He emptied Himself. So many people are waiting for God to empty us of bitterness, envy, hatred, malice and other toxins in our character and spirits. In truth, we have the power to empty ourselves of many of these things by simply recognizing them and refusing to submit to them. Since it is going to come out of us anyway, we may as well control where it goes.

If you are or have been a fleeing leader, are you empty of your old attributes? Have you poured yourself out or are you waiting for God to do it? Can you remember where you poured yourself out? If not, why not? Was it a spiritual experience or natural? Was God present when you poured yourself out? Who else was there? Did you pour into someone else in the process? Like Jacob, have you wrestled with God and yourself? Jacob had a limp – what is noticeably different about your character after encountering God? Have you confronted your Esau? Would your Esau agree that you are empty? Jesus made himself of no reputation – what reputation have you made for yourself? Christ took on the form of a bondservant –what form have you taken? When confronted with problems, do you flee or confront them? Have you really changed as a person or is Jacob wearing Israel's form?

6

A Man Such as I

Nehemiah asked a critical question when confronted by enemies trying to persuade him to abandon his God-given assignment, as well as the people entrusted to him. When confronted with a plot to kill him because of the work he was doing, he was presented the idea of running and hiding in the temple to save himself. His response to this notion, which will forever ring in my spirit was, "Should a man such as I flee?" This was not a question of arrogance or conceit but instead one of Godly character and responsibility. Nehemiah understood the mandate of God upon his life and the responsibility to preserve God's people over himself. When he pictured himself running for his own life and leaving the wall open and God's people vulnerable, it raised this question out of righteous indignation.

What kind of legacy is this for a man given a great work by God Himself to complete? How can someone given tremendous responsibility over God's children, as well as authority and favor over resources, flee for their own lives at the sign of personal attacks? Doesn't the scripture teach us "the good shepherd lays down His life for the sheep?"

It is the hireling who places his personal interest and preservation over the needs of God's people. Men like Nehemiah realize they are called to do what they place their hands to. Nehemiah did not need to rebuild the walls of Jerusalem for personal gain – the needs of the people and the work called him. He gave up his status and position with the king to become a servant leader to his people. Nehemiah used his own authority and influence to advance those who were in greater need than he was. His personal view of himself was intertwined with the needs of the people to whom he was tasked. The statement "a man such as I" is not a personal testament of greatness but rather the greatness of the individual responsibility he was given. This type of personal view calibrates successful leadership in the body of Christ. It is a mindset to maintain a spiritual character regardless of the circumstances one finds himself confronting. The ultimate act of laying one's life down for God's sheep starts with setting our lives aside for God's service. It is the true nature of our Chief Shepherd, Jesus Christ, when a leader puts himself in the place of those whom he leads. Christ left His heavenly estate and became like us so He could deliver us.

Nehemiah understood this inasmuch as he chose to put himself in the position of the remaining Israelites left in Jerusalem. When he arrived in Jerusalem and evaluated the devastation, he did not run from it but instead chose to live and lead in it. In chapter 2, he gathers the leaders together and says to them, "'You see the distress **we** are in, how Jerusalem lies waste, and its gates are burned with fire. Come and let **us** build the wall of Jerusalem, that **we** may no longer be a reproach.' And **I** told them of the hand of **my** God which had been good upon **me,** and also of the king's words that he had spoken to **me**. So **they** said, 'Let **us** rise up and build.' Then **they** set **their** hands to do this good work."

The ability of the best leaders to motivate people to accomplish a good work is inevitably tied to the leader's ability to place himself within the work. Effective leadership does not stand in safe places issuing commands but instead gets in the midst of a situation and leads through inspiration. We cannot lead people out of ghettos and slums without ever going in the ghettos and slums. If you want a person to come out of bad finances and debt, do not be afraid to "go there" in your own testimony. Too many contemporary leaders want to teach divine principles from ivory towers with no personal testimonials. The scripture reveals "we" overcome by the word of our testimony and the blood of the lamb! Rev. 12:11.

Self-denial is an essential ingredient in leading a people out of spiritual and physical places of oppression. Jesus declared that if anyone desired to come after Him one of the first character requirements would be self-denial. Any leader who has not developed a level of self-denial will doom himself and those who follow him. You cannot live in self-denial if you do not practice it, and you cannot effectively teach what you do not live.

How willing are you to place yourself in a person's situation as Jesus did with us? What moves your spirit to action as a leader? Why? How are you connected to it personally? What will you gain from it becoming successful? What does it mean to you to see other people built up? How does the despair of others affect you? Why do you believe you feel as you do?

The doom of those who follow this type of leadership is the student will effectively become like their teacher. Unbalanced, over-indulgent, self-righteous leaders inevitably teach people to be just like them. The church has recently become plagued with this type of leadership and doctrine, which will serve to destroy coming generations of believers if not corrected.

Unfortunately, the opportunities for leaders to exploit vulnerable people in ministry are frequent and broad. Many of God's people find themselves being further oppressed by the very people who are supposed to lead them to deliverance. Greedy leaders who do not understand they have been entrusted by God to preserve His people will exploit gullible souls. Peter wrote of false leaders who would "entice unstable souls" and "promise liberty while they themselves were slaves of corruption." 2 Peter 2:14-

19. Part of Jerusalem's prolonged devastation involved the remaining Israelite leaders taking advantage of their own people's oppression. The breaking of this cycle in Israel required a leader who fully embraced self-denial.

Nehemiah understood the depth of his leadership went beyond repairing the brokenness in Jerusalem's wall to the brokenness in Israel's people. He refused to receive the governor's portion that the former governors had imposed on the people. They had formerly laid burdens on them with no consideration of their state. Jesus issued the same indictment against the Pharisees when He said they "bind the people with heavy burdens but they themselves would not lift a finger." Not only did the governors exploit them, but the scripture says their servants did as well. Nehemiah knew the cycle of oppression had to stop, beginning with his leadership. Neither he nor his servants were allowed to take advantage of God's people in their oppressed condition. He even refused to purchase available lands because they rightfully belonged to the people who had been oppressed. This was extreme self-denial that was required of a man "such as this." His one request to God was "remember me, my God, for good, according to all that I have done for this people." Neh. 5:19.

Nehemiah's character and success was hitched to fact that he understood "the hand of the Lord had been good upon him." When a leader allows his relationship with God to regulate every desire and all of his decisions, it places him in a safe place character-wise. Understanding that God is "Jireh, our Provider" and operating in the character necessary to please Him always brings personal stability and prosperity. God Himself rewards righteous character. Too many contemporary leaders ditch righteous standards for a quick opportunity to make money regardless of the potential damage to the Body of Christ. The more an individual learns personal trust in God and His ability to provide before entering into leadership, the better leader they have a chance of becoming. Leadership of God's people should not be predicated on what we can receive from people but rather what we are called to offer them. Some of the greatest leadership opportunities come from refusing resources as Nehemiah did. Assessing the mindsets of the people who are giving is an important factor in leadership.

The apostle Paul revealed a lot of this in his teachings to the Corinthian church. Both the offerings received for the poorer Jerusalem churches and the rejection of personal compensation were done with a mindset of shaping the church's character. In our personal compensation as leaders, we must always consider the effect it is creating in the church culture.

By contrast, leaders not receiving proper remuneration can create an entitled mindset among members and a form of abuse of leadership. Scriptures reveal the student does have responsibility to "communicate" financial support to their teacher. False humility toward members can desensitize a congregation toward a leader's needs. Creating a mindset that congregants do not have a financial responsibility toward their leaders is equally as bad as leaders exploiting members. The key to all of it is divine balance, doing it the way God prescribed. Nehemiah and his leaders did not reject support, they simply maintained a standard that would not burden or exploit God's people. A healthy attitude toward money in the leader is important.

What are your beliefs about usury and exploitation? Do you truly understand God's position as it relates to the treatment of the poor? What value do you place on compensation in your service to the kingdom? How far will you go to be compensated? What are you willing to forego, if necessary? Would you walk away from ministry work if compensation were not involved?

> *How much self-denial have you made for the kingdom? Have you ever used or exploited anyone in ministry? How do you feel about it? If so, would you do it again? Why or why not?*

Imbalances as it relates to resources often occur when church leaders are exposed to more resources than they have ever managed or been exposed to personally. "Not many mighty or noble are called", but God actually chooses underexposed people so that He might get glory out of their lives. Problems occur with resources when individuals do not submit their financial affections to God as they lead His people. You can be a preacher and still have a personal struggle with money. In fact, this scenario is not uncommon. I have heard that statistically preachers and police officers are notoriously bad at managing personal debt. The rationale is their careers afford them a level of respect, which typically does not correlate with their compensation. Trying to make the two appear to match, they may overextend themselves financially with cars, homes and clothes beyond their pay grade. "Fake it until you make it" becomes the order of the day. Unfortunately, days become years, then decades and finally a lifetime of bad financial decisions. Countless amounts of hard-earned member resources wind up being flushed down tubes just to keep up appearances. In the end, it is allowed by God but not blessed because it lacks His divine nature. We still have free will! It epitomizes the spirit of the prodigal or wasteful son who squandered his inheritance. A pit stop in the pig pen served to be the deciding factor to facilitate his change of character and subsequent deliverance. He ran until he ran out of money and options. Unfortunately, leaders with this type of spirit continue fleecing sheep to the last member, if necessary. They often live one step above the pig pen while they drive everyone else there. The Nehemiah-style of leadership debunks these types of challenges because of proper prioritization. It is leadership which focuses on re-establishing foundational places in the lives of God's people. The heart to restore God's glory in the lives of His people overrides petty desires to appear great. Nehemiah-style leaders spend a lifetime of self-denial, bringing people back to stability and unity of the faith.

If you are or have served with a Nehemiah-style leader, God bless you. In today's society, the Body of Christ needs more sacrificial leaders like this. If you lack personal, Nehemiah-like character and are privileged to serve with this type of leader, glean all you can. You are in rare company!

Are you a Nehemiah-like leader or have you been privileged to serve with one? Whose life is more fortified because of your commitment to the kingdom? Do you believe God is pleased with your sacrifice? Would you want God to remember what you have done? Are you responsible for wasting resources or do you model and teach others to be good stewards? Does your leadership empower people or drain them? Does anyone receive the greater benefit of your service to them or do you?

7

What Are You Chasing, Gehazi?

In 2 Kings the story is told of the mighty Syrian general named Naaman being healed of leprosy by the word of the prophet Elisha. Not only was God revealing His sovereignty as the true and living God, but He was also establishing the authority of His servant Elisha to Naaman and both the kings of Israel and Syria. The king of Syria, a larger foe of Israel, determined to send one of his commanders to Israel to be healed of leprosy. Upon receipt of the letter from the Syrian king, the king of Israel tore his clothes in fear, realizing his natural authority was not enough to heal Naaman. He knew he needed divine power. The next verse reads, "So it was, when Elisha the man of God heard that the king of Israel had torn his clothes, that he sent to the king saying 'Why have you torn your clothes? Please let him come to me, and he shall know that there is a prophet in Israel.'" God was divinely orchestrating a situation so that all parties involved would discover His greatest authority did not abide with the political authority of the king but rather the spiritual authority of the prophet. It has not changed in today's society; God's ultimate authority does not lie in the hands of corrupt governors, senators or the president. The seal of God still abides with His prophets. Unfortunately, too many people are in the presence of prophetic authority treating it commonly.

When Naaman arrived in Israel at Elisha's door he expected to be regarded as nobility and treated like a great man. Instead, he was treated like a leper. Elisha never made any physical contact with him but simply sent instructions for him to dip himself in the Jordan River. I do not believe Elisha was being indignant, he was, however, offering Naaman total deliverance from his leprous condition and himself. Elisha did not feel the need to feed into Naaman's ego because he did not want anything from him. In addition, he was unwilling to sell out the character of his prophetic mantle to a glorified heathen. Too many of God's servants reduce their own anointing by exalting secular authority above divine authority. Prophets struggling with personal lust wind up compromising their divine positions for the recognition of people actually sent to them for deliverance. Whether it is political or business alliances, the prophetic mantle must be preserved from corruption at all times. No amount of money, status or personal connections should cause a prophet to lose his place in God. It is never worth it. Elisha understood this, unfortunately his servant Gehazi did not.

What authority do you value most, political, civil, business or spiritual? Why? What role does spiritual authority play in your life? How do you regard spiritual leaders? How do you believe God values them? Do your values match God's? Why or why not?

When Naaman left Elisha's home, his pride almost caused him to miss his deliverance. Fortunately, his servant offered him wisdom that effectively changed his life. By obeying the word of the prophet, he not only was healed of leprosy but came into the knowledge of God Almighty. On his return from the Jordan, he came back to the prophet with a different approach, greater respect, and a generous contribution. Elisha received everything from him but the financial gift. However, his servant Gehazi, was consumed with greed and thus made a critical mistake. The problem Gehazi faced was being in the same physical place but obviously not the same spiritual place as the prophet. He actually thought he had a better understanding than Elisha did. Many

What Are You Chasing, Gehazi?

people positioned with prophetic mantles miss the bigger picture because of what is in their heart. They unfortunately discover the significance of the anointing they are connected to when it is too late. Naaman came back from the Jordan River with clean skin and a clearer understanding of the prophet Elisha. After one personal experience, Naaman knew, beyond a doubt, that God was real and Elisha was His prophet. Gehazi spent all of his time with him yet had filthy desires in his flesh and no real understanding of whom he served. He actually was delusional enough to desire money over the anointing God had placed on Elisha's life. How blind can we be?

Do you understand your spiritual leader's worth? How valuable is what you gain from them? What else are you looking for? What's more important to you, what you desire or what you have received from them?

When Elisha refused Naaman's gift, Gehazi in his greedy thinking considered this as "sparing" him. Gehazi felt like Elisha was letting a big fish off the hook even though the prophet's spiritual assignment was complete. The two of them clearly were not on the same spiritual page. Inner greed and lust drives a person to always look for ways to get things from people. Any material opportunity, regardless of the spiritual ramifications, becomes the utmost priority. This type of person hates to feel like they missed an opportunity to squeeze out something, or receive something being offered, even if they do not need it. It is dark character, and very difficult to be cleansed because it reveals itself as light. Gehazi probably assumed that Elisha was not thinking about his needs when he refused Naaman and got the dark idea to take care of himself. Jesus said, "If the light in you is darkness, how great is that darkness?" Self-preservation becomes the order of the day, even if it means chasing after sinful ambitions.

So it was with Gehazi. He discarded the character of his divine assignment, the prophet he served, and all common decency. The scripture reveals when Naaman left Gehazi said, "As the Lord lives; I will run after him and get something from him." He literally ran him down by foot just to get his hands on a little bit of money. Unfortunately, I have seen the same spirit in ministry workers. Many people place little to no value on the spiritual deposits received from their proximity to God ordained leaders only to chase after a financial opportunity. The scripture depicted him as "Gehazi, the servant of the man of God" who was running after the insignificant trinkets in Naaman's chariot. What a pitiful image and waste of a divine investment. He left the wealth and character of the Kingdom to chase after a little bit of nothing. Unfortunately, he did not treasure the prophet's anointing or wisdom over material possessions. He thought he knew what was best for himself and the carnal desires of his heart dragged him behind that chariot on that fateful day. It was fateful because although he obtained what he pursued naturally, he also received more permanent things he neither desired nor expected. He positioned himself to be judged as opposed to being blessed.

Many followers serving in anointed places have Gehazi's dark character. No matter how close they may be to a leader's anointing, they cannot shake those inward desires. At the end of the day, they are chasing something. Whether it is wealth, a vision of themselves, unfulfilled childhood dreams, someone else's vision or lustful desires, the chase is never good. It always proves unsuccessful in the end because God never called us to chase anything. His sons are led by His Spirit. Being led requires a different mindset, disposition, level of patience and trust in God. The leading of God allows you to say no to anything that He has not prepared for you because He will not allow you to have peace with it. God's leadership gives you the grace and tact to know when to say yes

What Are You Chasing, Gehazi?

or no to opportunities. It does, however, require you to trust God and the people He places around you to have your best interest at heart. Self-preservation and greed will destroy that trust. Because self-preservation can masquerade as God's leading, followers have to be guided by several character questions.

Are your actions consistent with the character of Christ and your spiritual leader? Do you have to lie or deceive to achieve you ultimate goals? Does anyone have to be manipulated in the process of achieving your goals? Where do your decisions and actions leave you with the spiritual leader you have been called to serve?

If one or all of these questions are outside of God's character, you are not being led by God, you are chasing something.

Gehazi manipulated the situation, lied and misrepresented Elisha for the sum total of two talents of silver and two changes of clothes. After hiding the ill-conceived goods in his house, he tried to return to Elisha as though nothing happened. He was then asked three important questions by the prophet. First, *"Where have you been?"* The question infers that at some point Gehazi left them. I have discovered in ministry that people will leave and go other places. By this, I mean they will leave the spirit and character of a leader and church long before their physical departure takes place. Spiritually, they will go places which do not reflect the nature and spirit of place they are planted. When and if they return, they are dramatically affected by the places they have been. Apparently, Gehazi left Elisha long before Naaman arrived or he never would have chased his chariot. The second question Elisha asked him was far more profound. He asked, *"Did not my heart go with you?"* Note, he did not say spirit but rather heart. Gehazi could not go in the spirit of Elisha because his actions were corrupt from the start. To go in his spirit he would have had to align with Elijah's character and nature.

No one can operate in the spirit of any leader who refuses to align with the leader's nature. If he had done this, he would not have chased Naaman's chariot. When Gehazi reached Naaman he pretended to be there in Elisha's spirit and it worked on the foreigner because he didn't know the prophet's nature well enough. Anyone that truly knew Elisha would have suspected something was wrong. I have seen members from churches where I am familiar with the pastor and you can tell immediately if they have the leader's spirit. It is like someone pretending to be a person's child – it does not feel right! If you talk to or spend time with them you'll discover they're not related in spirit. You can, however, go with a leader's heart even though you do not have their spirit. A leader's heart is their deep concern and compassion for a person's well-being. Elisha was trying to convey his love for Gehazi and that he truly wanted the best for him. Whether Gehazi received it or not, Elisha had not only invested time in him but also his heart.

Followers frequently leave churches and leaders erroneously carrying a pastor's heart with them. A leader will allow his heart to go where his spirit will not. Your biological children can go away from your home in wrong ways, not carrying the spirit of your family, but your heart for them will be right there. The prodigal son left home with a little bit of his father's money and a lot of his father's heart. While wallowing in the pig pen he did not carry his father's spirit but still had his heart. When Gehazi took the money from Naaman he disappointed his spiritual father's heart.

What Are You Chasing, Gehazi?

If you serve with a God-given leader, do you have their spirit? How do you know? If not, why not? Whose spirit do you have? If you answered God, you have a problem! Are you suggesting no one can cover or disciple you but God? How about your leader's heart? Do you believe you have it? Why or why not? Have you taken their heart somewhere it should not be?

In the third and final question he asked, "*Was it time to accept money and garments?*" Greed and lust want immediate gratification and will distort God's will for a person's life. Solomon wrote in Ecclesiastes 3, "There is a time and season for everything under the sun." When you are chasing things, you inevitably get ahead of predestined seasons. In effect, you become your own god. Elisha, hearing from God, knew it was not time to accept material things but the time would come. However, the burning greed in Gehazi would not allow him to submit to God's divine leading through Elisha. His out-of-control desires doomed him. *Are your desires submitted to the will and timing of God? Or, do you decide when it's time to bless yourself? Would you submit to your leader's direction for your personal decisions?*

All of these answers have consequences associated with them. The consequences for Gehazi were much farther reaching than he could have imagined. Because he refused the spirit of Elisha, he in turn received a large portion of the spirit he was chasing. Naaman left with Elisha's spirit of worship and placed his new values there. He wanted to be forgiven for having to escort his master into a false place of worship, though it was his job. As a result, he chose to no longer carry the spirit of Syria. He desired the dirt of Israel to be carried back with him to enact holy worship unto God. His new nature literally placed more value on holy ground than money. On the other hand, Gehazi was seeking a portion of Naaman's old, dirty values when he came seeking money. Unfortunately, those values came with a "generous dose" of leprosy as well. Be advised; when you chase things, you are subject to catch everything that comes with them. Not only did Gehazi get the money he sought, be he also received enough leprosy to spread from him to all of his succeeding generations. The prophet pronounced the leprosy would cling to him and his generations forever. This is a sad commentary for a man who served a prophet with the power to heal. I am sure his appreciation for Elisha's anointing changed when he saw himself covered with leprosy, knowing the prophet's word could have delivered him if his heart was right. In the end, I wonder if he felt his chase was worth what he caught?

If you are discovering you are a person who is chasing something, have you truly considered what you may catch? What are you chasing and why? Can you live with the negative effect of your goals? Has your heart left the place where you serve? Can you come back? What will return with you? Have you already gone too far? How do you know? What have you caught?

8

Five Stones....Five Enemies

When following a leader who is anointed you must be mature enough to understand the power of the anointing to preserve the people surrounding it. However, other leaders and followers benefitting from the anointing should do everything Godly possible to preserve it and the individual it rests upon as well. In 2 Samuel 21:15, a second giant and descendant of Goliath of Gath came seeking vengeance against Israel. A much older but anointed David went to fight yet another giant for God's people. In the midst of the battle David grew faint and the giant, Ishbi Benob seized the opening to kill David. The Bible describes the enemy as having a new sword, which is translated in Hebrew language as "a new thing."

Many years earlier in the initial battle against Goliath, a younger David chose five smooth stones to war against the giant. It only took the hurling of one of those stones to overcome the mighty giant on that day. At the end of the battle, David dropped the remaining four stones but picked up four new giant enemies in spirit and flesh. The scriptures reveal three other giants in addition to Ishbi Benob, all of whom were descendants of Goliath, came looking for David at some point. This is an interesting correlation to consider, five stones versus not one, but five giants. Though David fought and killed one giant on the field of battle, the four others were still alive. Long after the four remaining smooth stones were dropped and Goliath's head was severed, four more enormous enemies lived with the dream of killing David. Here is a spiritual principle to consider – the anointing which destroys enemies also produces enemies. As sure as an anointed leader defeats one enemy, the devil will raise up another with a "new thing." There will be a new lie, new tactic, new person with a new agenda and a new attack as long as an anointing is present! However, even the greatest of men carrying the most powerful anointing will eventually grow weary. After all, they are human. Scripture teaches even young lions grow weary. We have a tendency to burn out our brightest leaders by putting them at the forefront of every battle. I have seen people bring every problem that exists in and around the church to the pastor as though no one else is capable of handling anything. We set good leaders up to become faint and overexposed to enemies through needless battles. Many pastors could receive fresh visions, sermons and do "greater works" as Christ said if they were not so battle fatigued.

As David grew faint in battle and Ishbi Benob moved in to kill him with his "new thing," one of David's leaders named Abishai came to his aid and killed the giant. Fortunately, the rest of the leaders were wise enough to realize the nation could not afford to lose the anointing upon his life. They called David the "Lamp of Israel," meaning God was bringing the light of prosperity to Israel through him. The risk of losing David was far too great, so the secondary leaders all agreed to fight future battles in his stead. In all, David's servants killed four additional giants of the Philistines, making a total of five including Goliath. That is one for David and four for his leaders. In the end, David and four of his spiritual descendants warred against Goliath and four of his giant descendants. Four fresh new stones fought against four new giants.

At some point, supporting leadership should catch the spirit and anointing of the head and be able to contend against new spirits which descend from old ones. Fresh new "lively" stones should be raised up in our churches for the sole purpose of fending off enemies sniping at the anointing. In addition, every new tare, which joins the church, should not so easily access and frustrate the anointing God is using to bless the Body. There should be a band of submitted leaders who have a mindset and spirit of preservation surrounding the leader. *As a member, how much are*

Five Stones....Five Enemies

you willing to put on the line for an anointing that covers you? I constantly hear many people frivolously talk about receiving an anointing like an accessory to their wardrobe. Rarely do I see people willing to serve an anointing by putting themselves in sacrificial positions. Note this; <u>you will never receive an anointing from God if you are unwilling to serve an anointing sent from God.</u>

God will not position you to lead under an anointing if you cannot remain in position under anointed leadership. Every great anointed leader in scripture had an anointed leader, of some sort, who trained them in their anointing. Moses submitted himself to Jethro, and later, Joshua was called Moses' minister. Joshua could not have led the nation of Israel had he not have served Moses. Elisha had to follow Elijah and the famed, mighty men had to follow David. The twelve disciples had to follow Jesus for three years sacrificing everything just to be in position to receive His anointing.

I have to admit my personal frustration in watching a generation of "wannabe" leaders who dream of thousands of God's people following them yet they cannot successfully serve one of God's leaders. In my pastorate, I have been favored to grow a church to thousands of members, but I assure you it could not have been done without the lessons learned serving other leaders. God has given the anointing to accomplish the work but knowing others have faced and defeated giants gives me confidence in my battles. The added benefit of helping other great men is gaining the knowledge that I too need help. I realize there is no way for me to effectively handle the weight of my ministry without the support of genuine followers. However, followers cannot be unwilling to be trained by my anointing. Like David's leaders, those who fight in a leader's stead should do so in an effort to preserve the leader's anointing as opposed to developing their own. Inevitably, serving another leader will foster personal development, but should this be the primary goal of the servant? If you use someone else's fight to establish your own identity you, in effect, become a new adversary. By this, I mean your character is proven untrustworthy because you are using the leader's vulnerability to promote your own strength. In fact, your strength should be used to eliminate the leader's vulnerability. No one fighting for a leader should have it in their heart to eliminate the leader. The fight should be to preserve the leader and cause for which you fight. The leader's identity or place should never be in question by the ones fighting or watching. If an individual stands in a leader's place, there should be a sincere undertone of "we cannot afford to lose you." If you do not feel this in your heart, you may be unintentionally acting as a replacement to a leader.

This was the dilemma created between Saul and David. When David entered the battle zone under the barrage of insults lobbed by his brother, he asked one critical question – "Is there not a cause?" 1 Sam. 17:29. The fact is there really were two questions that needed to be asked. Goliath had campaigned for one man in Israel to come out and fight for the honor of their nation for forty days. King Saul and the entire army were camped opposite the Philistine and his army for the entire period, yet no one moved. Fear crippled the entire Israelite army for the same period of time it took God to cleanse the earth of unrighteousness during the days of Noah. God was able to wash the entire earth in forty days, yet not able to compel an Israelite male to fight for their God's honor in the same period of time. Unfortunately, King Saul was in the number as well. Therefore, the second important question to be asked was, "Is there not a leader?" Was there not someone identified by God to lead the nation at a critical time like this? If so, why wasn't he out there confronting Goliath for the cause of God and His country? Preserving a leader means that those who fight in his stead should not have to do anything the leader is unwilling or afraid to do.

You cannot preserve leaders in areas where they will not lead; instead, you produce new leaders in those areas. Saul's attempt to dress David in his armor was meaningless due to the fact his cowardice loomed larger than his leadership. There was nothing left of his leadership for David to preserve – the king was afraid to use his own armor. When David stepped on the battle field in Saul's absence versus his stead, it began the process of him becoming Saul's replacement. Though David's intent was pure, Saul's leadership void made them unintended rivals. It would be impossible for the army and nation to view David as a secondary leader to Saul after David defeated a giant, which Saul was clearly afraid to fight. Unfortunately, Saul had never lead or trained David in battle; instead, David trained him in a sense. When David courageously stepped on the battlefield winding a sling as he ran toward Goliath, the nation was watching the emergence of new leadership as opposed to an extension of Saul's leadership. I cannot imagine that David was thinking, "We can't afford to lose our leader." There was no leader to lose – the king was hiding on the sideline with the rest of the soldiers! Unfortunately, David was tasked with showing an army how to fight for a God cause in the absence of leadership. As a result, Saul's cowardice could not absorb David's courage. Therefore, the two would unfortunately be viewed as independent leaders from this point forward.

Unintended or deliberately, are you an independent leader in your church? Can you honestly say you are an extension of the leadership you serve? When you are being used in ministries in your church, have you taken time to examine the motives of your heart? What is your attitude toward the preservation or elimination of your leader?

Honest answers to these questions could serve to resolve many conflicts in your life and potentially the church as well.

For example, are you the associate minister waiting for the opportunity to preach and reveal the difference in your style and revelation as opposed to your pastor? Or, do you hope the uniqueness of your gift will serve to support and enhance the message the under shepherd is trying to convey to the body?

Be honest with yourself. In either case, your gift can be used but toward what agenda? One agenda serves your own interest while the other serves to preserve your leader and the cause they are working toward. Subtle, selfish thoughts reveal our true motives. The rejection of thoughts like "we can't afford to lose your anointing at this time" reveals inward malice. The person who usually harbors this type of malice will often appease themselves with words like "God doesn't need any of us." This is a subtle attempt to equalize leaders and followers. When a follower says this to a leader, it is a form of arrogance. No matter how smoothly or self-righteously it is done, it is usually a malicious jab.

By contrast, a leader saying it to a follower is typically a demonstration of humility designed to encourage and/or teach. For example, you would not say to a president of a nation, "You are a citizen just like me and this country will move on without either of us." Though he is a citizen, in truth he is not just like you. His role is more vital to the nation than yours is and his absence would serve to have a greater impact on masses of people. Making the statement to the person occupying the office would demonstrate utter contempt and disrespect. However, self-pride and arrogance completely blinds this type of person to reality. In contrast, if the president said, "I am a citizen like you and we all have our roles to play," the individual is demonstrating humility by stating a truth without being specific.

When David's mighty men essentially said, "We can't afford to lose your anointing," it demonstrated a sober view toward him, themselves, the nation and God. They were not being idolatrous, but rather unselfish and movement focused. A person drunk on himself would have a problem making the same statement. In large part, it would be due to a lack of respect for the anointing they serve and an over regard for their own. David's mighty men served as eliminators of the problems that confronted him as opposed to hindrances to the work he was accomplishing for the kingdom. They became co-giant slayers by serving and following the original giant slayer. They saw something in him that God apparently valued so they chose to value it as well. Four mighty men became fresh living stones for David to hurl at the new giants who confronted him in later years. I believe he was able to launch the living stones with the same confidence he held in the inanimate stone which toppled Goliath. Regardless of your position in church, can your leader point you in a direction with the confidence that you will overcome shared adversities?

Is your character rock-solid enough to be used in a trial without falling apart with your own independent agenda? Can you be considered a stone in the hand of a capable leader facing tremendous problems? If released, do you have the character weight to arrive at the destination intended by the leader? Or, would you veer off course and hit the marks you deem more vital to your personal objective, leaving David exposed and vulnerable?

9

Who Killed Uriah?

A good leader should never allow bad character choices to place good followers in destructive situations. It is understandable when the devil causes problems in the Kingdom and good men have to place their lives on the line, but it is an entirely different thing when a leader's poor decisions and carnal desires place followers' lives at stake. So was the case with David and one of his best soldiers named Uriah. You could not have found a better stone in the hands of David than Uriah. His character, commitment and loyalty to the kingdom and his king were unrivaled. He was the kind of man any leader would love to have on his side and deserved to be treated honorably. Instead, he was destroyed by his own leader's deceit. Unfortunately, he is not alone. Many modern leaders do not realize the devastation that poor character can cause in a follower's soul, spirit and ultimately their life. I have seen people all but give up on God and the church after discovering their leader was living a double life. As leader's we must understand that not only are our public decisions critical to ministry, but our private ones are as well. Nothing about our private lives should detract from our public ministries. A good leader should not have to resort to hiding and covering up his actions done in private. Our lifestyle decisions and choices should always reflect the integrity of the God we serve as opposed to burning acts of flesh. Too bad David did not follow this principle; it might have saved Uriah's life. Even as greater leader as David was, he too became subject to sin.

Most of us know the story of David walking on his balcony seeing the beautiful Bathsheba bathing on her roof top. Overcome with lust, he decides to lay with her, at all cost. It did not matter to the king that she was married to one of the most loyal soldiers at his disposal. He was blinded by his lust. In a moment of heated passion and poor judgment, David makes a singular decision, which will ultimately destroy a good man's life. There was no coming back from sleeping with Uriah's wife. To make matters worse, the woman became pregnant with the king's child. Now David is left with two potential directions to travel. Either stop, turn around and accept responsibility for his actions or continue driving down the dark road of deceit. Unfortunately, he decided to drive.

Many contemporary leaders make the same wrong decision to continue driving forward in sin until they are caught. Hoping to fix problems secretly, they wind up making matters worse. The word says, "If we confess our sins, God is faithful and just to forgive and cleanse us from all unrighteousness." 1 John 1:9 It is always better to confess than to keep producing more mess. You cannot fix old deceit with new deceit. The unwillingness to confess reveals inward distrust of God's faithfulness. Why do we allow our hearts to distrust God when we fail? He is not unfaithful, we are!

David comes up with the devilish idea to involve Uriah in his deceit versus exposing his mistake to him. He calls the soldier in from the battlefield, looks him in his face and lies to him. For the king's devious plan to work, there had to be a crack in Uriah's character. Many times, someone else in leadership has to be complicit to a leader's bad decisions and poor character. For example, if a pastor is sleeping around or stealing money, someone else usually knows about it. It may be a secretary, financial assistant or armor bearer but usually someone knowingly or unwittingly is dragged into these types of messes. *So it is not only the leader, but also what follower's character flaws have to be exploited in order to achieve the primary leader's deceit? Who else knows about the deception but will not say anything? Who has been brought into the poor character position of the leader they are following?*

Who Killed Uriah?

Paul said to the Corinthian church, "Follow me as I follow Christ." Notice he did not only say, "follow me" but "as I follow Christ." A good leader should never coerce innocent followers to join them in personal sins. We should never exploit sin in the people we are called to lead and deliver from sin. It is bad enough to commit the sin but it may be worse to compel God's flock to participate with you.

If you are a leader committing personal sins, how many followers are involved? How did they get involved? What kind of example are you setting? Whose character flaws are being exploited by following you in sin? What do you perceive will be the outcome? If discovered, how will it affect their lives? Can you live with the outcome?

David thought he could exploit Uriah but he was never more wrong about anything! Uriah's name means, "The flame of Jah." This is interpreted the "fire of the Lord most sacred and vehement." It means Uriah lived with one of the most sacred and passionate types of fire in his heart for God. This type of passion does not douse easily, no matter whom you are following. When following greatness, this type of person can inspire a leader. However, when following corruption the same person will expose a leader.

David devised a plan for Uriah to take a break from battle, hoping he would go home and sleep with his beautiful wife. The soldier's character or conscience would not allow him to do it so he slept by the king's door instead. He refused to break rank like his king because his heart was with God and the army back on the battlefield. When David awoke to find his plan was shot, he asked Uriah why he did not go home. His response should have broken the corrupt character of the king. He said, "The ark and Israel and

Judah are dwelling in tents, and my lord Joab and the servants of my lord are encamped in the open fields. Shall I then go to my house to eat and drink, and to lie with my wife? As you live, as your soul lives, I will not do this thing." Wow! Talk about a follower's character exposing a leader's corrupt heart! He essentially told David the presence of God and His armies were on the battlefield where the king should have been. He then asks the king how could he go home and eat, drink and be with his wife at a time like this. Furthermore, he expressed loyalty to David by stating he would not do it as long as David lived. How could David possibly continue in his deceit after hearing this response? Not only did he continue, he drove deeper in sin!

I am fully convinced that most over-the-top sins do not happen without God giving multiple ways of escape along the way. The scripture reveals, "There is no temptation that overtakes a man except that which is common. And with the temptation, God will provide a way of escape." 1 Cor. 10:13 David could have escaped his sins several times but chose leadership assassination instead. This is when a follower's actions are more righteous and threaten to expose a leader's unrighteousness. Rather than own up to the character flaws, the leader uses his authority to destroy the follower.

Like Uriah, many people do not make it back from this type of attack. Their spirits are often crushed and they choose not to pursue leadership roles anymore. They do not die physically but something dies in their spirit toward leading and leaders as well. No leader should ever stoop to this depth, but unfortunately, many do. If David, "the man after God's own heart" did, what makes you think other leaders will not? David devised a situation to place Uriah on the front line in the heat of battle knowing he would be killed. Being a master of war, he not only knew that he would be killed but how violently as well. To make matters worse, he trusted Uriah to deliver his own suicide mission unopened to his commander, Joab. The message read, "Set Uriah in the forefront of the hottest battle, and retreat from him, that he may be struck down and die." 2 Sam. 11:15 This was beyond deceitful, it was evil! Not only would David be guilty of betrayal and murder, he found the crack in Joab's character to make him complicit.

As I previously stated, leaders are rarely alone in their corruption – they usually have to involve someone else in their deceit. The scripture reads, "So it was, while Joab besieged the city, that he assigned Uriah to a place where he knew there were valiant men. Then the men of the city came out and fought with Joab. And some of the people of the servants of David fell; and Uriah the Hittite died also." 2 Sam. 11:16. Tragically, Uriah was a vital person in David's hands who was totally betrayed by his leader. In fact, he was so faithful when given the suicidal command; he marched to his death without hesitation. Talk about having the stone-like character to complete your leader's requests! Too bad the leader's character did not match the follower's. Do not be mistaken, David was still a great man but he made an even greater mistake. It was the kind of mistake which required God Himself to step in and handle the leader. "Be not deceived, God is not mocked, whatsoever a man sows that shall he reap also." Gal. 6:7. Do not be fooled, David paid dearly for his sin. There was no way he could continue serving the righteous God and this kind of character be overlooked.

Every leader who misuses God's flock will eventually confront the consequences of their actions. It is better to turn yourself in. The Bible says, "It's a fearful thing to be in the hands of an angry God." Heb. 10:31.

If you are a leader, do your actions merit the type of people committed to your leadership? How much value do you place on their lives? What are your boundaries? Is there a Bathsheba moment in your life? How about Uriah? Have you ever committed leadership assassination? How many of God's people have you killed? If exposed, how would your private life affect your public leadership? If your answer is not good, who else have you involved? Is there a Joab who does your dirt for you? What would the effect of your exposure be on them? What is the effect of your leadership on them? Can you live with the consequences of your leadership? Who killed Uriah, the enemies, Joab or David?

10

Thank God for Nathan

Confrontation! This is what God required the prophet Nathan to do to cause King David to recognize his sin. Not dance around the issue, avoid it, pretend like nothing happened or tell himself it was not his business. Plain and simple, God called Nathan to confront David about his sin! One spiritual leader had to confront another spiritual leader about the effect his personal sin had on his leadership and the people following him.

It is not at all uncommon in the scripture. Jesus constantly confronted the Pharisees, especially with the "woes" of Matthew 23 where He openly called them hypocrites. He also confronted the greedy money changers in the temple which led to Him turning over tables and driving them out with a whip of cords. Paul confronted Peter "to his face" according to Galatians 2:14 because of his hypocrisy toward the Gentiles when Jewish disciples came around. An imprisoned John the Baptist confronted Jesus by messengers when he asked "are you the one or should we believe for another?" Luke 7:19 From the Old Testament to the New, I could name countless acts of God-led confrontation which typically resulted in re-establishing divine order and personal relationships. Yet, the contemporary church, and primarily its leaders, flee from it like Old Testament leprosy! I am not suggesting turning over tables and grabbing whips, but some sins cannot be avoided, they must be confronted.

The key to successful confrontation among leaders is addressing issues as representatives of spiritual principles instead of acting like adversaries. It is not personal, it is the Kingdom. When one spiritual leader has to confront another, it is not about who they are but rather Who they both represent. We are mouthpieces for

God, "in season and out of season." We are called to speak up for Him and cannot be parties to His name being dishonored, no matter who is involved. The Lord revealed if we are ashamed to honor Him before men, He will not honor us before the Father.

Beyond shame, the other critical aspect of spiritual confrontation is courage. I have discovered many pastors and ministers struggle with cowardice. Whether it is fear of losing jobs, status, money, friendships, support of people, etc. many leaders cower at the idea of confrontation and learn to live with their fears. As a result, the devil finds ways to torment them because 1 John 4:18 reveals "fear involves torment." In other words, wherever the spirit of fear exists the enemy finds a way to attach some form of emotional or spiritual torment. Whether it is inner torment from the guilt of disobeying God or the external torment of people who should have been corrected, cowards will not have peace. I know this because God loves us too much to allow us to live peacefully as cowards because it is a sinful nature. "God has not given us a spirit of fear." 2 Tim. 1:7. Revelation 21:8 reveals that cowards will be thrown in the lake of fire along with unbelievers, murderers, liars and the sexually immoral. A believer can no more be at peace as a coward than they could as liar, murderer or adulterer. According to Paul's instruction to Timothy, leaders/teachers are held to a "stricter judgment." We as leaders, more than others, cannot be cowards.

How much does cowardice factor into your leadership character? Do you avoid confrontation? Do you have to be involved personally to confront an issue? Have you ever confronted an issue on principle? If it is not your responsibility, whose is it? Are you representing God or yourself? How far are you willing to go in representing God? What are you willing to lose for God? What are you not willing to lose? Given your responses are honest, would you define yourself as courageous or cowardly?

I thank God Nathan was not a coward! It took great courage and wisdom to obey God in confronting David about his sin with Bathsheba and the subsequent murder of Uriah. Chapter 12 of 2 Samuel begins with a short but powerfully poignant sentence. It reads, "Then the Lord sent Nathan to David." To fully comprehend the dramatic tension of this statement, we have to highlight the last sentence of chapter 11. It reads, "But the thing that David had done displeased the Lord." As we all know, the thing that David had done was committing adultery with a man's wife then having the man murdered. Most people would have taken one of several positions. 1) He is the king, who am I to get in the middle of that mess? 2) It is their business; I am not in the middle of it! 3) It is done, no one else knows so leave it alone! 4) God will take care of it! God sure did take care of it with a leader named Nathan!

Can you imagine the fear and paranoia Nathan had to overcome to prepare himself to confront David? After all, David had already murdered Uriah in cold blood. On top of it, he used his authority to do it in a stealth way, so why would he not do the same to Nathan? One reason, **God sent Nathan to David**! Beyond his human emotions, Nathan had the security of knowing God was sending him to do this assignment. Moreover, because God sent him, He had already prepared David's heart to receive him.

This is very important for any person reading this chapter who believes it is their responsibility to fix every leader in the Body they perceive to be wrong. Remember this principle – when men commit sin, God sends men to reveal sin! <u>You cannot go to men in sin until God sends you.</u> Otherwise, you will not be received. However, when God does send an individual to deal with sin, it is not the time to become a coward! In moments like this, an individual becomes God's mouthpiece as Moses was to Pharaoh. Therefore, the words of your mouth must be seasoned with salt and layered in wisdom. It is not a time to simply speak, it is more important to be heard.

David heard Nathan because he used wisdom and the skillful words, which God had given him. The first wise thing he did was paint a picture to David of the sinful principles he committed with no particular personality attached to it. In other words, he pointed out the situation without pointing at the man. This took a great degree of emotional control and personal detachment. There was not a need to highlight the man in sin but rather reveal the situation as sin.

When we are immature and overly emotional, we make issues more about the person than the act of sin committed. Then the individual involved becomes more consumed by what is perceived as a personal attack or agenda. When sin is clearly seen as sin, a person cannot help seeing themselves entangled in it. Nathan wisely kept it at a level of principle; it never became personal until David asked who the person was in the story. Then Nathan courageously told David, "You are the man." He did not play with it or avoid it, he did what he was "sent" there to do! He did not allow himself to be gripped and beset by a cowardly spirit, he spoke up for God. Let the chips fall where they may but his job was done. Because of Nathan's courage, David had a profound confession out of which came some of the most profound scriptures of repentance in Psalms 51. 2 Samuel 12:13 reads, "So David said to Nathan, 'I have sinned against the Lord.'" Then in Psalm 51 he wrote, "Against thee, thee only, have I sinned." Nevertheless, he first realized and confessed it to Nathan through the courage he displayed in exposing the sin.

How many leaders and people caught in sins have missed their moments of deliverance and revelation because someone who was sent to them would not speak for God? How many testimonies and stories of restoration has the Body of Christ missed because of a cowardly spirit as it relates to confrontation?

Thank God for Nathan

I am reminded of the question God asked in Isaiah's presence in the sixth chapter of his book – "Who will go for Us?" Prior to Isaiah's request to be sent, he had a revelation as well. In God's presence, he discovered that he was unclean, and he dwelled amidst an unclean people, yet he was willing to be cleaned personally and then become an agent to reveal to others how to become clean. His "going" was not for himself, it was for God.

We are living in a time of profound uncleanness in the church as well as the world. An unclean church cannot deliver an unclean world! The Word teaches us that judgment begins in the Lord's house, and it starts with leadership. Like Isaiah, someone has to accept being cleaned and declare what being clean is to others! Contrary to popular opinion and political correctness, there is a wise and respectful way to address leadership which has fallen into overt sin. We cannot hide from our God-given assignments and prop up cowardice as a virtue. If you are afraid or immature in confrontation, confess it. It is the first step to deliverance. We cannot continue to allow the Lord and the Kingdom's character to be demeaned by open sin. The blood will be on our hands as well because our silence becomes consent.

Study the examples in scripture and pray for wise and practical approaches if there is not a model before you. The Spirit of the Lord will guide you in this as He does in everything else. Anytime you feel alone in your assignment, like no one else understands, read 2 Samuel 12 and then thank God for Nathan!

Do you believe you have developed Nathan's type of wisdom to confront an issue? Why or why not? What personal examples do you have? What was the end result of your confrontation? Was it a God result? What could you have done differently? Did you allow your emotions to interfere? Are you presently avoiding confrontation? Why? Is God sending you or not? How do you know? What are your confirmations? What if you are wrong?

Can you receive confrontation? Why or why not? When confronted with your own sins, how do you respond? Who do you represent, God or yourself?

It is also interesting to note that Nathan was in the kingdom with David and had access to him but was not an insider. It is most difficult for someone directly under someone's leadership to correct a leader. Affection and respect sometimes cloud the judgment of followers as it relates to good leaders. After all, David was God's man who did an unusual and terrible thing. Someone close to him would have had a difficult time processing his mistake, even as egregious as it was. God's wisdom usually selects someone like Nathan, not directly accountable to him, who can come and go when necessary. David was a king/priest over the nation but Nathan was a prophet. His sole responsibility was to represent God, and David understood this when he heard him say, "You are the man." It was as though God Himself had uttered the words to David, because the man who said it was that connected to God. Few others could have pinned David like this even with wisdom and skill. It is important that leaders like Nathan do not run in cliques and circles but allow themselves to be known as God's truth tellers. It does not matter who they speak to because they have no agenda but God's. They are always available to speak truth to power because they are not angling for anything or trying to position themselves. He was already positioned as, "Nathan, the prophet of God." It was enough for him.

John the Baptist was a New Testament example of this when he spoke to Herod about his salacious affair with his own niece. Everyone else saw it, but John had the courage to say something about it. It literally got his head cut off, but it did not matter, he had done his job. Jesus did not rescue John from prison but rather paid homage to him by saying that among those born of a woman there was "none greater" than John. These were mighty words from the Savior about a man who essentially came to Israel with a message of confrontation. Similarly, John and Nathan appeared to live simple and somewhat isolated lives. John left the comforts of the city to spend his time in the wilderness. Nathan left the exposure and comforts of David's house to return to his own home. The last verse in chapter 12 reads, "Then Nathan returned to his house." No hype or fanfare, just a man of God going back to his own home alone. We hear nothing else about him as it relates to this because we did not need to – his job was done. It was never about him, it was always about God's will being done. Sounds like Jesus, doesn't it – "Nevertheless, not my will but thine be done." Christ also came and did His job and went back home without fanfare. It is the prevailing theme of men called to speak for God – be prepared to be effective but not celebrated. If you have a strong need to be celebrated, you are emotionally unprepared for spiritual confrontation.

11

The Spirit of Diotrephes is in the Church

In John's third epistle, which was addressed to Gaius, he raises an issue with a particular leader in the church whose character was causing an inordinate amount of trouble. His name was Diotrephes, and his spirit was clearly and distinctly a problem in the church. John describes him by saying, "I wrote to the church but Diotrephes, who loves to have preeminence among them, does not receive us." The idea of preeminence means he was selfish, self-centered, self-seeking and always wanted to be considered first. Unlike Christ, he did not desire to serve but rather be served.

Diotrephes can be found in almost any church. They may be the worship leader who only has an excitement for worshipping God when they are leading worship services. If anyone else is leading the worship service, it is not good enough for Diotrephes to stand, join in songs and clap their hands or even act interested. In their mind, they are the only one able to do it properly, so why participate? He can be the associate minister who only gets excited about the Word when he is preaching. Diotrephes can be the sister who has to put every special program together and subsequently tells everyone how much work it took during the service. Or the secretary who retypes every letter from auxiliaries because no one else's writing will meet her approval. The deacon who keeps all the church keys, the checkbook and has to be consulted for every minor thing in the church can be Diotrephes. He can be found in the lead usher who causes everyone to wait until they arrive to pass out fans, programs and then stands in the most prominent spot to be seen by others.

If this spirit is in any form of leadership in your church, you have a major problem! Much like Diotrephes resisted John; this spirit will wreak havoc and fight against leadership just to be seen. Individuals like this have no regard for righteousness but rather have a spirit of "I'm rightness." He is, at the end of the day, a self-centered bully! This type of individual takes advantage of the docile nature of God's sheep knowing that they are not inclined to resist. Diotrephes will stomp around the church like a bull in a china closet as long as there is no one strong enough to restrain him. He is a weak pastor's nightmare! The spirit can come in the form of a deacon, lay member, choir director, minister or even a pastor's wife.

In the south, I have seen it on more than a few occasions operating in a so-called deacon's board. Note, I did not say deacon's ministry but rather a pseudo board of people who are supposed to be servants. Using the term deacon's board is like saying waiter's board, janitor's board or valet parker's board! Imagine going to a restaurant and having to consult a board of waiters to get approval to sit at a table and hope they will allow you to eat. What if you had to go through a waiter's board instead of notifying your individual server every time you made changes to your menu items? Suppose the waiter consistently came back to the table and told you, "Most of the board was in favor of you having the grilled chicken but the head waiter did not agree, so it will not be possible." How long or how many times do you suppose you would endure this before becoming disgusted and lose interest? The food would absolutely have to be heavenly and virtually impossible to find on earth to keep sound-minded people going there. This is the ridiculous culture created in churches with boards which have to approve every little nitpicky thing pertaining to member needs. We wonder why churches like these are unable to grow, and the members who remain are all sitting on some type of board.

Servants are supposed to facilitate the needs of others; they do not sit on boards. The first seven deacons in the book of Acts were selected for the sole purpose of serving the needs of the saints and relieving the apostles of those types of burdens. They literally waited tables for the Palestinian and Grecian widows in their daily distribution of food. The ministry of the deacons was to serve the needs of people who could not serve themselves. Deacon's board members, however, view themselves as overseers and lords, and it becomes a prime place to foster Diotrephes' spirit. He will typically be the strongest-willed and most influential character in the pack and at some point will cause weak men to fear resisting him regardless of their convictions. He will oppress members as Diotrephes did in John's epistle and make everything in the culture about himself. The needs of others will be minimized and at the end of the day – everyone else will exist to serve the needs of Diotrephes.

Have you experienced a Diotrephes' spirit in church? How does your attitude compare to his? Would others say that you have his spirit? Are you a servant or do you desire to be served? How willing are you to cooperate with others? What does having a title mean to you? How badly do you desire to be recognized? What happens when you are not? What are you willing to do to be recognized?

I am discovering the spirit of Diotrephes has recently risen among pastors who actually believe the church and its members exist to serve them in any offshoot personal desire. This new phenomenon of pastors, Christian artists, etc. shamelessly promoting themselves in everything known to man is akin to Diotrephes loving to have preeminence among the saints. I understand the use of marketing and branding in limited doses for the development of churches, ministries and Christian organizations. However, we are hard pressed to go a day without receiving some piece of church literature, advertisement, e-blast, Facebook ad or text picture without an oversized picture of pastors looming somewhere on the page.

For example, some leaders will go as far as putting overly affectionate types of poses of themselves with their spouse on a flyer announcing something as simple as a church car wash. For example, why would the honeymoon picture of the pastor and first lady be on a flyer inviting surrounding churches to their choir's five-year anniversary and concert? What are we to interpret from this image? Could it be their unique and profound love for each other is going to release a special anointing on the service which people cannot afford to miss? Are they suggesting that their loving affection for one another has been the inspiration and guide for the choir to remain together for years? Or, could it be they want everyone to know who they are, having lost all sense of boundaries and seizing every opportunity to promote themselves, even if it is inappropriate. At any rate, it is far too sensational and self-serving for a Kingdom comprised of servants.

In business, this type of thing is not done because it has considered unprofessional or tacky. An advertisement should highlight the product not the person, unless the person is the product. Anything otherwise speaks something to the readers about the individuals who put the advertisement together. It suggests a lack of the social graces necessary to know the boundaries between promoting an event versus promoting yourself through an event. If it is repugnant in secular business circles, it is downright deplorable in the church community. Unfortunately, the church community has, in effect, become more competitive than business circles. We, as Christian leaders, seem to have lost all sense of divine boundaries for the sake of being personally recognized. We anxiously, almost narcissistically, want to show what we are doing even when it is not anything of major significance or distinction. In fact, what is being done is typically not more than most and far less than some. The major difference is who is doing it; therefore, everyone has to know about it. We claim to use promotions to win sinners but most of our promotion is sent to other churches. Is the true purpose to reach the lost or trying to show ourselves to be progressive and ahead of others?

John said it – Diotrephes just had to be first among all the other saints. I wonder what percentage of church announcements actually make it into the hands of unbelievers versus other church members? We once held a large concert only to come outside and find a local church had placed flyers on all of the cars inviting people to their worship services. As I picked up one of the many discarded invitations littering our parking lot, I could not help thinking of the waste of Kingdom resources and time. Imagine, someone took the time to place cards on hundreds of cars in an effort to win converted believers to their church. At the same time, there probably were a dozen or more nightclubs open with more people and cars gathered in their parking lots. I wondered if the workers considered visiting those parking lots. Which group do you think needed to visit their church the most, the church crowd or the club crowd?

Some things are a waste of Kingdom pearls and time. The competitive desire to be the biggest and best will sometimes blind us to simple Christian ethics. Never waste your time trying to compete with other churches or leaders. Not only is this profoundly distracting, it will corrupt your heart as well. Do not compromise the Christian standard God's grace has privileged you to be a part of to promote your own name or agenda. In the end, you will lose far more than you could ever gain. Though it may have become popular, it is neither right nor worth it!

As a leader, what are your boundaries in self-promotion? Would you compromise the church's image to promote yourself? Do you feel the need to compete with other leaders? Why? What will you gain if you obtain your objective? How important is it to you? Will it sustain you eternally?

Another profoundly alarming trend is the concept of the church regarding the Pastor's birthday like the first and second coming of Jesus. We are not talking about simply cutting cake, going to a restaurant or passing out a few gifts but rather elaborate and costly endeavors. I understand honoring a servant, but if the honor washes out your servant-hood and makes you the served, you have lost your view of Christ. Some of these birthday celebrations have gotten so far out of hand, that the churches will actually do more for the pastor and first lady's birthday than honoring the birth of Christ. Before some readers nervously blow too many fuses, be reminded, I hold the office of Senior Pastor. I currently oversee and financially support six churches and understand exactly what I am stating and the ramifications of it. I am certainly not talking about dishonoring God's servants or robbing them of their well-deserved "double honor." No one wants to be dishonored, but there is a fine line between honor and vainglory. I would also remind us the scripture tells us "the servant is not greater than his master." I was alarmed to hear many churches had week-long services for the "man of God's" birthday one year but closed the church doors on the observance of the Son of God's birthday. The excuse was Christmas fell on a Sunday and people wanted to spend time with their families. Apparently, the pastors were fine with it so the worship of God was cancelled on Christ's acknowledged "birthday."

This sounds like "worshipping and serving the creature rather than the creator" to me as it says in Romans 1. The scripture also reads, "Although they knew Him as God, they neither glorified Him as God nor were they thankful." If you are a pastor reading this book and these circumstances took place in your church, you took preeminence over Jesus! Becoming angry for pointing it out to you will not help, instead, repent and return your attention to your First Love. The Bible says, "Do the first works all over again." Let us make it all about Jesus! If the spirit of Diotrephes is going to effectively be dealt with in followers, it certainly cannot exist in leaders.

Do you believe you deserve to be honored? Why? What if God and scripture don't agree with your approach to honor? Whose job is it to reward you, the body of Christ or the Lord Himself? What happens if the body does not show you the honor you believe you deserve? What are you willing to do to gain it? Do you believe this would please God? What are you unwilling to do? Why?

The final characteristic scripture reveals about Diotrephes, which is sometimes found in followers, is prating against leaders. To prate means to "bubble up" or "talk junk" as we call it in the south. No follower should be comfortable "talking junk" to any leader. You could not think of this kind of insubordination in the U.S. military – imagine how wrong it is in God's army. This level of offense would cause you to lose rank or receive a dishonorable discharge, depending on the severity of the offense. Anyone openly prating in church requires the disciplinary attention of the leader. John said Diotrephes did it with malicious words and intent. In other words, he was spreading evil statements about leadership in the church. Proverbs 8:14 says, "God hates those who sow discord among the brethren." Something is very wrong with individuals spending an inordinate amount of time digging up and hurling evil accusations at spiritual leadership. A true Christian is not going to be comfortable with this conduct, even when the individual is guilty. Scripture says, "Satan is the accuser of the brethren."

If you believe a situation is so bad, properly confront it or remove yourself. Many times, you will find people in church creating an atmosphere of openly talking negatively throughout the congregation about a particular leader. Even if the accusations are true, there is a proper way to confront an elder. When done improperly, it does not help anyone but simply sows discord among the brethren. Collectively, God calls this a murmuring spirit and it is one, which He did not take lightly with Israel. In fact, it so offended God, He killed droves of people who committed the act during the exodus just to make the point. People talking junk about the church, vision and leadership can cause a lot of things to be killed in ministry.

When Diotrephes is allowed to prate, it also causes sincere people to avoid becoming part of a congregation. Most people have enough confusion to tend to in their own lives and do not enjoy meddling in God's affairs, however, if not rooted out, Diotrephes will embolden messy people to become like him. They will kill the spirit of the innocent and immature and drive away good brethren. This is why John determined to confront him when he came to the church. As a leader, you cannot tolerate nor facilitate the spirit of Diotrephes in any capacity. As John stated, his deeds cannot be overlooked, they must be "called to mind." Not only must they be called to Diotrephes' mind, but all those affected by him as well. Open rebellion calls for open rebuke! Paul taught in his epistles, "Rebuke those who are sinning openly so the rest may hear." Openly rooting out praters silences all of the whispering and murmuring produced by the spirit. The Bible reveals that the righteous are as bold as a lion. The required response to a prating Diotrephes is the boldness of the lion, not the meekness of the lamb! Too many innocent sheep are at stake for a leader to be meek with open rebellion. Like Jesus, our job is to protect God's flock. We cannot be self-preservationist.

Are you a person inclined to prate like Diotrephes? How do you handle things when you do not agree with them? Who do you talk to? What is your attitude toward spiritual leadership you do not agree with? As a leader, how do you deal with people who prate openly? What is your willingness to confront and "call to mind" their actions? Why or why not? Are you inclined to protect others or are you a self-preservationist? Would others agree with your answers? Who have you preserved other than yourself? Would Diotrephes call you a self-preservationist or a protector of others?

12

Who Will Give You Your Own?

In Luke 16, Jesus asked," If you have not been faithful in what is another man's, who will give you your own?" I want to take a little time to examine some of the profound principles in this question. The first issue to be raised is faithfulness and to whom or what it pertains. In 1 Corinthians 4, Paul says, "Moreover it is required in stewards that one be found faithful."

In the examination of faithfulness through Jesus' question and Paul's statement, I will start with the word "moreover." It essentially means "more than everything else." More than talent, gifting, abilities, charisma, popularity and all the things contemporary leaders seem to place great value upon. Paul says this is the one thing "required" of stewards. By definition, stewards are those to whom something has been given, therefore every blood-bought, spirit-filled believer of Jesus Christ is a Kingdom steward. Any and everything that comes from God's Kingdom belongs to Him and is released to us through stewardship. If whatever you have or do pertains to or comes from God, you are considered a steward of God's possessions.

Paul said the one character trait, above everything else a steward must have in his possession, is that he is "required" to "be found" faithful. It is important to understand Paul did not only say **be faithful** but rather **be found faithful.** This means a steward cannot determine his own level of faithfulness, someone else does. God does not give us the authority to promote ourselves based on our perception of works we deem faithful but instead puts us in position to be deemed faithful or unfaithful by the one who is leading you. If you are saved, you will spend your entire life serving God but in the end Christ will determine if your work was "well done." Regardless of how you feel about it, it is His decision because the work you are doing pertains to Him and He started first. He said, "Upon this rock I build my church and the gates of hell shall not prevail against it." Jesus gave the vision of the church's origin and completion. If you only do what you desire in the church versus what He wants done, you are not doing well in Christ's eyes, and His opinion counts more than yours. He has the right to call you unfaithful in the things that pertain to Him.

A clear example of this is all the people caught in the judgment of Luke 13 who are called workers of iniquity. In the eyes of Christ, a worker of iniquity is an individual who works in a spiritual atmosphere toward the goal of satisfying his or her own flesh. They are self-willed as opposed to being spiritually motivated. This individual takes Christ's Kingdom for granted and leads himself or herself in God's work as opposed to seeking Christ or His leaders for God's will for themselves and the church. As a result, they are known for doing things in the name of Christ but unfortunately are not known by Christ. It does not mean that Christ is unaware of them; they just refuse to be in relationship with Him. They enjoy holding on to the things of God rather than being embraced by God Himself. It is virtually impossible for this type of person to follow spiritual leadership because they refuse to follow the Holy Spirit. As a result, Christ rejects them as sons and daughters because Romans 8:14 reveals, "As many as are led of the Spirit of God, **these** are the sons of God." It is real clear, no leading of the Holy Spirit in earth, no eternal sonship in heaven. It really is a shame because the person gets a weird sense of enjoyment from being in God's presence in worship service – they just hate to be led by God in their daily lives. Like the people in Luke 13, they are content with being hearers of the word but never become doers.

This is why Christ's question about being faithful to that which pertains to another man is being brought into view. In the Kingdom, you do not "get" what you want – you receive what He wills for you. However, you can only receive based on that which you are willing to give. The Word says, "Whatsoever a man sows, that also shall he reap." To "get" implies taking or grabbing hold of something by strength, might or ability. Receiving something places authority and power in the hand of the one who is giving to you.

> *How willing are you to give your strength to someone else who is called to lead and develop your anointing, character and abilities? How much energy do you give towards developing the things that pertain to them? As good as you feel about your service and commitment, what do they have to say about your work? How do you receive correction or instruction from leaders? Whose opinion matters the most to you – yours or theirs? Whose opinion do you think matters the most to God – yours or the steward to whom He gave the authority and responsibility?*

This is the place I have seen trip up many secondary leaders such as ministers, deacons, choir directors, etc. They really believe that God values their views and opinions over someone God has made a steward of His possessions and people. Would that not make them the leader instead of the follower? Amazingly, church seems to be the primary place people like this tend to test their theories. Somehow, they find ways to restrain themselves at work with disagreeable bosses and hateful co-workers trying to discourage them into quitting. For the sake of a paycheck, individuals will overcome every obstacle and endure hardness as good soldiers and not allow themselves to even consider quitting. When it comes to Christ and His spiritual bosses and co-workers however, it becomes a radically different story. The level of endurance and tolerance seems to dramatically change when it comes to being spiritually rewarded for faithfulness. Quitting is not only an option; it usually becomes the first choice! If not quitting, then rebelling against leadership with no concern or fear of what the potential recourse could be.

How well do you endure for the sake of spiritual assignments? How easily do you quit spiritual assignments? Have you ever left a spiritual assignment incomplete? How did it affect the church? Do you believe it affected you? Will it affect you in the future? What do you believe the Lord's assessment of your work will be?

Many secondary leaders, in fact, become so dissatisfied they believe the time comes for them to "get" their own church or ministry. This is not only true of church but business and all sorts of things which require us to follow someone else's lead. *Here is the question Jesus essentially asked – if you were unwilling to give yourself to someone else's vision, who will give themselves to yours?* The inference in Jesus' question about faithfulness when He asks "who will give you your own" is that your own cannot be gotten, it must be given. Jesus said to the disciples, "To you it has been given to know the mysteries of the Kingdom." You cannot get revelation from God by might and power, it must be given and received by the Holy Spirit. You cannot get anything spiritual from God, it must be given.

I have seen people wanting to start a church go out and get a building using their money, get chairs, microphones, put up a sign and call it a church. A church is not something you simply start somewhere in the earth with a building, chairs and a sign. It is a mysterious revelation of God which begins in heaven and must be received in earth. God deems those who are faithful enough in the earth to be called stewards of His mysteries and revelations. This is what Paul was referring to in 1 Corinthians when he talked

Who Will Give You Your Own?

about being stewards of the mysteries of God. Man looks at the outward, but God who looks at the heart, calls and chooses those whom He deems faithful, then He gives them a revelation of Christ, His gospel and His church. Upon receiving the revelation, they are sent by God as Romans 10:13 asks, "How can they preach, unless they are sent?" God does not send anyone for Him who works to kill the ones He has already sent.

According to the parables that Jesus gave us, God takes away from those who reject His servants and dishonor His son. In the parable of the landowner with the vineyard in Mark 12:1, the landowner (God) leases His vineyard to wicked vinedressers (Israel) and sends His servants (prophets) to collect fruit in due season. Instead of rendering fruit to the servants, they beat, stoned and killed those whom He sent. Finally, He sends His son (Jesus) and they kill Him and try to take His inheritance by force. The landowner destroys the wicked vinedressers miserably and gives or leases the vineyard to new vinedressers who will render the fruit in due season. The new vinedressers are the stewards of the church who must be faithful to give God what He wants, when He wants it. But just like the old vinedressers, He expects the new to respond respectfully to the servants He sends to collect His fruit. Plain and simple, God will not give you a vineyard to dress when you have been unfaithful and disrespectful in a previous vineyard. I did not say you could not go and get one, I said He will not give you one. But when He does come to your vineyard, expect it to be destroyed miserably, if not given by Him. I've watched ministers like this go out and get churches only to have them and their lives thrown into chaos as well the people blind enough to follow them. The principles of God cannot be circumvented or escaped. If you could do this, it would make you greater than God!

If you are a leader, were you given a vineyard or did you get one on your own? Are there any of God's servants you have disrespected in the past? Would God's servants agree with you? Who have you served who can vouch for your character? Do you believe you will reap what you have sown? Do you want to reap what you have sown or would you prefer forgiveness?

Too many people believe their gifts and abilities should outweigh poor character and unfaithfulness and God should bless them in spite of themselves. Consider this: He loved Israel and He broke off their branch according to Romans 11. Christ was the only begotten Son of God, and He allowed Him to die on the cross for our sins! Paul wrote in Romans 11:21, "For God did not spare the natural branches neither will he spare you." *How expendable do you believe we are in the divine equation?*

I am concerned about this contemporary reckless disregard for God and His Word many people have when they discover something they want or feel they should do. Not only will they do it, but carelessly put God's name on it when it reflects none of the character or standards of God. In short, they are guilty of attempting to reduce God to the level of their desires as opposed to allowing Him to reveal and raise their standards to the level of His will. Paul said in Romans 1:22, "Their foolish hearts became darkened. Professing to be wise they became fools and changed the image of the incorruptible God into an image made like corruptible man." Translation: they thought so much of themselves, sinful men tried to convince the world that God looked like them in sin instead of seeking to become righteous like God. When trying to discover if you are following God, take a good look at all attributes of your life. If your life looks like His Word, then He is leading you, if not, something else is driving you!

Who Will Give You Your Own?

As leaders, many things attack our minds, soul and spirits trying to draw, entice and drag us out of the will of God. If we do not keep God's Word as a measuring stick for our spiritual growth, sin and corruption will inevitably dwarf us. We will become overcome by sin and not even know it because our language still sounds spiritual. The problem is, however, the words source from earth rather than heaven. I am growing tired of hearing fleshy, earthly jargon wrapped in spiritual-sounding clichés being pawned off as a word from God. Too often, it is distant and very poor exegesis of anything remotely considered to stem from the heart of God. People use carnal statements like "you've got to sow where you want to go." It sounds good in the flesh, but it is a road to spiritual disobedience, a lot of wasted time and lost resources.

The first problem with the statement is the irreverent disregard for God's plan for your life. This is carnal minded – do whatever you want and call it God-language versus being led by the Spirit. It essentially says, "Decide where you want to be and give enough money to get there!" Never mind God's will for your life. What if your desire is to go one direction and the Spirit desires another? Remember, you are not your own, you were bought with a price. Where you want to go is of little relevance to God, you were saved for His will, not your own. Even Jesus submitted His own will to the obedience of the Father! That little bit of spiritual leaven could destroy your destiny and purpose by your own doing, not the devil.

The word says, "My people are destroyed for lack of knowledge." We base the credibility of the words like this on "who" is saying it rather than "what" God has actually said in His Word. Scripture says, "Let God be true and every man a liar." Every man, no matter how great or small must be measured against the Word of God. We are hearing messages in the earth from people God has not sent yet, supposedly declaring a word to God's people. The Bible calls this false prophecy. Do not be fooled; the devil is still a very good liar. His best lies, in fact, convince people that he is not the devil nor is he lying! If what you are hearing is not reflected in God's word, it is not truth even if you liked what you heard.

Leaders must learn to measure themselves by the truth of God's word rather than what we feel may be true about ourselves. We hear what others have said about us, enjoy it, imagine ourselves in it, and then offer it up to God as a pseudo prayer of faith for His will in our lives. It typically is not His will but rather our own and it is a form of self-deception. Unfortunately, many leaders walk in self-deception being blinded by their own darkness and unable to see or receive the glory of God. If they did receive His glory, they would not give it to Him; they would heap it upon themselves instead! Therefore, God refuses to give them visions of His will for ministry because they would turn His kingdom into their own empire. Leaders like this do not think like stewards but rather as emperors. Thus, we have so many leaders searching for and chasing people who have the material image of success. Others confer and bestow false blessings upon themselves because they cannot receive anything from God.

The word teaches that double-minded men are unstable in all of their ways and cannot even expect to receive anything from God. Their desires are out of the earth, so the people they pursue do not have to possess any fruit of the Spirit or divine attributes of God, just be materially blessed. The entire focus shifts from holiness and righteousness to favor and blessings.

What do you desire most from God, material or spiritual blessings? If you received everything you desire materially, how would you glorify God with it? Are you sure He would be glorified? How is He glorified through your current stewardship? How well do you follow the Spirit when His direction is not your will? Would God call you His steward or your own emperor?

Who Will Give You Your Own?

In Isaiah 3, a form of judgment came upon the nation where God took away all of the spiritual leaders of character and left them with children and babes to rule over them. It talked about the people being so oppressed that a man would take hold of his brother and make him a ruler simply because of the clothes he wore. I have seen pastors call men their spiritual leaders, not because of anointing but tailored suits and fancy cars. In Isaiah, their leaders were in ruins as much as they were, and many are still in ruins today. A great many spiritual leaders are thinking and acting like children. Little attention is paid to primary responsibilities, and childish desires stemming from selfish ambitions become the priority. Whole churches wind up following blinded leaders down paths to nowhere. As the scriptures have said, "The blind lead the blind." In discovering leaders versus emperors, there are significant questions that must be asked and answered.

Who are we following and what is his character? Where are we going? How will we know when we have arrived at God's destination? What will we do when we get there? What type of people will be there with us? Who will receive the glory?

A leader with a vision from God will have no problem answering these types of questions. Not every part of the vision may be detailed to the nth degree, but it should be plain enough to read and follow. To follow a leader in the anointing of God, he must have received an anointing from God. Anointing, revelations and blessings come from obedience to God and righteous living before God. This type of leadership is required to manifest a vision from God and bring His people to a place of holiness and blessings. It can only come from the Holy Spirit who is the Teacher, Comforter and Guide. Whether He is manifested in a vision, a sermon coming through the mouth of a servant, a business strategy being given to the Body, or the gift of leadership being exhibited by a primary leader, it should still be done in the character of the Holy Spirit. He is still leading Christ's church in the earth through physical men. Make sure God receives the glory in everything you do, and continue to follow His Spirit and His leaders!

About the Author

Eric Warren Davis is founder and Senior Pastor of Word of God Church and Ministries International. Since 2000, the membership has grown from thirty to thousands. They are currently housed at Word of God Dutch Square campus in Columbia, South Carolina. In addition to the Dutch Square campus, he has established WOG Español located at a second Southeast campus in Columbia. A third location located on 74 acres in Bishopville, South Carolina was acquired in 2007 for ministry retreats. The ministry has extended beyond South Carolina to establish WOGCM Baltimore, Ghana, Sierra Leone and Mexico. The movement encompasses various outreaches to include an Economic Development Center which houses a business park and multiple businesses such as Thrift Stores, Hair Supply store, Rental/Flower Shop etc. which generates revenue for outreach ministries and missions. A Community Development Corporation named God Cares, was also formed to provide relief and deliverance to individuals within our communities.

Pastor Davis graduated from South Carolina State University where he received a Bachelor's of Science Degree in Electrical Engineering Technology in 1991. He worked as a corporate engineer in the mid 90's prior to receiving his call in ministry and later, an entrepreneur. He developed outreach ministries and organizations in the greater Columbia area prior to becoming pastor of WOGCM. In 2008, he received certification in Executive Leadership from Cornell University. He is an experienced leader in both ministry and business and is considered a forward thinker in the area of social entrepreneurship which provides economic solutions to both Christian and social issues.

Pastor Davis is married to Vanessa Davis and God has blessed them with three sons – Ezra, Elias and Emmanuel. He is a committed husband, father and pastor.